THE ESSENTIAL GUIDE TO
GUIDE TO
TEACHING NEW
APPRENTICESHIPS

SAGE was founded in 1965 by Sara Miller McCune to support the dissemination of usable knowledge by publishing innovative and high-quality research and teaching content. Today, we publish over 900 journals, including those of more than 400 learned societies, more than 800 new books per year, and a growing range of library products including archives, data, case studies, reports, and video. SAGE remains majority-owned by our founder, and after Sara's lifetime will become owned by a charitable trust that secures our continued independence.

Los Angeles | London | New Delhi | Singapore | Washington DC

THE ESSENTIAL GUIDE TO GUIDE TO TEACHING NEW APPRENTICESHIPS

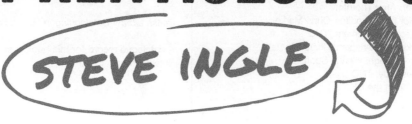

STEVE INGLE

LM Learning Matters

Learning Matters
A SAGE Publishing Company
1 Oliver's Yard
55 City Road
London EC1Y 1SP

SAGE Publications Inc.
2455 Teller Road
Thousand Oaks, California 91320

SAGE Publications India Pvt Ltd
B 1/I 1 Mohan Cooperative Industrial Area
Mathura Road
New Delhi 110 044

SAGE Publications Asia-Pacific Pte Ltd
3 Church Street
#10-04 Samsung Hub
Singapore 049483

Editor: Amy Thornton
Senior project editor: Chris Marke
Project management: TNQ
Marketing manager: Dilhara Attygalle
Cover design: Wendy Scott
Typeset by: TNQ
Printed in the UK

Library of Congress Control Number: 2020951558

British Library Cataloguing in Publication Data

A catalogue record for this book is available from the
British Library

ISBN 978-1-5297-4431-6
ISBN 978-1-5297-4430-9 (pbk)

At SAGE we take sustainability seriously. Most of our products are printed in the UK using FSC papers and
boards. When we print overseas we ensure sustainable papers are used as measured by the PREPS grading
system. We undertake an annual audit to monitor our sustainability.

For Kieran

CONTENTS

ACKNOWLEDGEMENTS

My most grateful thanks to all those who have contributed their time, ideas and inspiration in shaping this text for the benefit of other practitioners.

In particular, thanks go to:

Jo Brodrick

Sue Martin

Julie Gibson

Vicky Duckworth

Clive Cheetham

Jenny Coogan

John Daley

INTRODUCTION

If I have seen further it is by standing on the shoulders of giants

Isaac Newton

This book is designed to support all stakeholders who are involved with the planning, delivery and assessment of learners on the new, standards-based apprenticeships. You might be a teacher or trainer, a learning mentor or training consultant, an employer, supervisor or line manager. Perhaps you are just making the switch from working in industry to a new role supporting learners with their own development and progress, as they learn the new knowledge and skills needed to progress in their career.

The structure of the book and how to use it

Whatever your role, this book will provide you with valuable guidance on how best to support, challenge and develop learners throughout their apprenticeship journey at all levels. This book is divided into a number of key chapters:

Chapter 1: *An introduction to the new apprenticeships* – get to grips with the current apprenticeship model with a brief history of development, the transition from frameworks to standards, what is involved in delivering and assessing a new apprenticeship, and information on key organisations that can support you.

Chapter 2: *Programme planning* – ensuring individual apprentices get the best possible programme of learning that will be key to their success. This chapter explores the importance of finding out about your learners' starting points and how to build an apprenticeship programme that will really work for them.

Chapter 3: *Effective apprenticeship teaching and training* – an apprenticeship is not just about assessing what learners can do. The new apprenticeship standards require each learner to develop substantial new knowledge, skills and behaviours. This chapter explores some of the most effective approaches to really develop apprentices from their different starting points.

Chapter 4: *Ongoing assessment for vocational learners* – this chapter explores some of the best ongoing, formative, assessment practices to help you understand the progress that apprentices are making and where further development and support is required. This will ensure that your apprentices are well prepared to undertake their formal end-point assessments successfully.

Chapter 5: *Progress monitoring, personal development and target setting* – apprentices are also employees and need to carry out their work roles as well as learning new skills and juggling their busy personal lives. This chapter explores some of the key considerations in helping and supporting your apprentices to stay on track, keep motivated and overcome any barriers to learning they may face.

Chapter 6: *Meeting the requirements of high-quality apprenticeships* – this chapter explores the importance of quality, consistency and professional development. Ensuring your apprentices benefit from the highest quality training and support will help them to achieve their educational goals and meet the expectations of their employers. We will explore the expectations of high-quality apprenticeship provision, the role of quality assurance organisations and the education inspection framework.

Feel free to explore each chapter in order as it follows the apprenticeship journey. Alternatively, you may prefer to dip into each chapter as and when you need it.

The book is written to be accessible, supportive and useful. Whilst information is focused on the current apprenticeship system in England, those supporting apprentices in Wales, Scotland and Northern Ireland, or internationally, will still find the content useful. Each chapter features a number of key features to help you develop, grow and learn. These features include the following:

Reflection points – take a few moments to reflect on key issues and concepts and how they relate to your own professional practice, whatever your role in the apprenticeship journey.

Case studies – a specific look at how things are working in practice, from an apprentice, trainer, coach or employer perspective.

Take it further – ideas to challenge your knowledge and understand further by taking your learning to a deeper level if this is relevant to your role and context.

Find out more – links to good quality information and guidance to support your own independent research in a particular area.

1

AN INTRODUCTION TO THE NEW APPRENTICESHIPS

apprentice, n. and adj.

A learner of a craft; one who is bound by legal agreement to serve an employer in the exercise of some handicraft, art, trade, or profession, for a certain number of years, with a view to learn its details and duties, in which the employer is reciprocally bound to instruct.

Oxford English Dictionary

IN THIS CHAPTER

In this chapter you will learn about:

- the development of apprenticeships over time
- definitions of vocational learning
- the apprenticeship journey from agreeing a standard to end-point assessment (EPA)
- the different roles and organisations involved with delivering and assessing new apprenticeships

What is an apprenticeship?

Ask ten different people what an apprenticeship means to them and you may get ten different responses! One area they might agree on, however, is that apprenticeships are about helping someone to learn something new. In this regard, the real essence of an apprenticeship has remained unchanged since its introduction back in the Middle Ages. Various professionals have explored the history of apprenticeships in England (Evans, 2011; Mirza-Davies, 2015; Armitage and Cogger, 2019), highlighting a number of key milestones in the development of apprentice programmes as we might know them today:

The Middle Ages–1900: Contracts were drawn up between young apprentices and their 'Masters' working in the medieval guilds of trade and craftsmen, for example weavers, candlemakers, tanners, masons, cobblers and bookbinders. Once an apprenticeship was complete, sometimes lasting up to seven years, young apprentices could progress to become a 'journeyman', earning a wage for their skilled work, on their way to becoming an experienced Master craftsman themselves. This arrangement for 'time-served' training and experience in a given trade was formalised in law in 1563, with 'The Statute of Artificers', sometimes known as the Statute of Apprentices.

1900–1992: Apprenticeships became more wide ranging in occupations such as shipbuilding, plumbing and electrical work. By the 1960s, it was estimated that a third of boys leaving school went on to an apprenticeship. However, concerns over the quality of apprenticeship training began to increase with criticisms from trade unions and employers' associations that apprenticeships focused too much on the length of time served rather than the development of apprentices' skills through high-quality training and development.

1993–2010: A steep decline in the number of apprentices promoted government reform and the introduction of the 'Modern Apprenticeship', which focused on the achievement of qualifications such as national vocation qualifications (NVQs) rather than time served. The new millennium brought further changes as minimum standards were introduced with 'Intermediate Apprenticeships' becoming available at Level 2 (GCSE level) and 'Advanced Apprenticeships' at Level 3 (GCE A-level).

Young apprenticeship programmes were introduced to appeal to 14–16-year-olds at school, who were looking for more engaging, work-related, study options. The upper age limit of 25 was removed, making an apprenticeship a possible training route open to all. The 'National Apprenticeship Week' was introduced in 2007, as a way to highlight the apprenticeship route as a valid alternative to other more academic qualifications and pathways.

2010–2014: Higher Apprenticeships were first introduced in 2010 to provide a progression route to study at levels 4 and 5, followed by degree level apprenticeships in 2015, at levels 6 and 7 equivalent to qualifications available in universities and higher education institutions. In a bid to improve quality, the government set a minimum apprenticeship duration of one year, along with the requirement for apprentices to develop their English and mathematics skills if they had not already achieved a minimum GCSE standard on leaving school.

Various government reports and reviews into vocational learning also helped to shape the development of apprenticeship reforms in England. These include the Tomlinson Report (2004), the Letich Report on Skills (2006) and Professor Alison Wolf's (2011) Review of Vocational Education. In 2012, the government commissioned entrepreneur and educator Doug Richard to carry out an independent review of the apprenticeship system, to address ongoing concerns about quality and the impact of apprenticeships to meet employer's needs and the country's skills gaps.

The Richard Review of Apprenticeships (2012) proposed a number of important recommendations aimed at improving the overall quality and status of apprenticeships. These included redesigning apprenticeships around set industry standards which reflected the needs of employers, the importance of valid and reliable independent assessment at the end of an apprenticeship, and significant changes to the funding arrangements for apprenticeships. Richard's recommendations began to shape the government's apprenticeship reform programme and the new employer-designed apprenticeship system we have today.

2015–present: In 2015, the government published its 'Apprenticeships (in England): vision for 2020', including an aspiration to create 3 million apprenticeships by 2020. In 2016, the Report of the Independent Panel on Technical Education, chaired by Lord Sainsbury, and the OECD report on Building Skills for All (2016) provided a number of further recommendations affecting apprenticeships and technical and vocational education more broadly. And so began a significant transition away from the previous apprenticeship 'framework' system that had been delivered since the introduction of the Apprenticeships, Skills, Children and Learning Act in 2009, towards the new apprenticeships.

From frameworks to standards

The Specification of Apprenticeship Standards for England (SASE) set out the framework of competencies that apprentices used to have to complete, in order to achieve their full apprenticeship qualification. SASE frameworks were designed to prepare learners for work in a range of different occupations in a given sector area, for example business administration, customer service, hospitality or health care.

Apprentices were required to complete a range of different qualifications and components assessed throughout their learning programme, which included:

- achievement of competency and technical knowledge qualifications, such as NVQs and BTECS

- personal learning and thinking skills (PLTS)

- employee rights and responsibilities

- relevant English, maths and information and communication technology (ICT) qualifications, where required.

Although many apprentices were able to successfully complete and achieve their frameworks, there was often criticism from employers that these programmes were not fit for purpose. As highlighted in the Richard Review (2012) employers argued that learners did not always develop the skills and behaviours needed to perform a specific job role successfully. SASE frameworks had not been designed by employers and were often seen as a collection of different qualifications and competencies that did little to meet the specific needs of businesses and their workforce.

In response to these criticisms, the very first employer-designed apprenticeship standards were introduced, following close consultation with employer and stakeholder groups known as 'trailblazers'. A trailblazer group brought together a group of employers who reflected the broad range of large and small companies who employ people in a given occupation. Each group is required to have a least ten different employers, including smaller businesses, who represented the size and spread of their sector. Together, along with representation from relevant professional bodies and trade associations, they worked to develop the 'standard'; the minimum knowledge, skills and behaviours (KSBs) that an

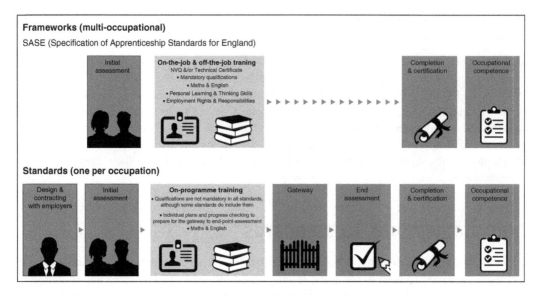

Figure 1.1 The new apprenticeship journey (reproduced with kind permission from 'Delivering Apprenticeship Standards', Education and Training Foundation. Available at: https://api.excellencegateway.org.uk/resource/etf:2326)

apprentice would need to be able to demonstrate by the end of their learning programme, to show mastery of their occupation. After development by the trailblazer groups, a 'route panel' of industry experts ensures that each standard is fit for purpose, before apprentices can be recruited and trained.

Figure 1.1 shows some of the key differences in approach between the older SASE framework apprenticeships and the new employer-designed apprenticeship standards.

The apprenticeship levy

To help meet the government's target to expand the number of new apprenticeships significantly, the apprenticeship levy was introduced in 2017, as a way to support the funding of apprenticeship training for all employers. Large employers, with a pay bill of over £3 million, are required to pay a levy of 0.5 per cent of their total annual pay bill. Organisations can access these funds, through their apprenticeship service accounts, to train new employees, or to upskill existing staff as long as the individual requires significant new KSBs to be occupationally competent in the job role.

Funds raised through the levy are also used to support apprenticeship training costs for smaller businesses who are required to pay 5 per cent towards the funding of training. If an employer has fewer than 50 employees, the government will pay all the costs of apprenticeship training, but the employer must pay at least the relevant national minimum wage to the apprentice depending on their age and the year of apprenticeship training they are in. Employers must also pay for any benefits and travel costs for their apprentices and release them to undertake their off-the-job (OffTJ) training entitlement.

Making the transition

So, although the general notion of an apprenticeship has been around for hundreds of years, the format, approach, composition, funding and learning focus have all changed considerably. This rest of book focuses on the **new apprenticeships**, and how best to ensure they are delivered effectively. You may be very experienced in delivering and supporting apprentices on the old SASE frameworks, you might be working with some apprentices completing a framework and others just starting a standards programme or you may be getting to grips with apprenticeships for the very first time.

The last date for new apprentices to start on framework programmes was July 2020, to complete no later than July 2025. If you are working with learners completing framework style apprenticeships, this book is also designed to help prepare you for the full transition to employer-designed standards apprenticeships.

Apprenticeships today

As we have explored, an apprenticeship can be simply defined today as a job with a formal programme of training. Today's apprentices are employed and received a salary. They work alongside experienced staff and participate in both 'on-the-job' and 'off-the-job' training, to gain the skills and competences needed by employers to carry out a specific role, for example a plumber, an IT technician, a team leader or a bus driver.

Today's apprenticeships must be designed to meet the government's funding rules and requirements for both employers and training providers. These requirements are laid out in the government's regularly updated apprenticeship funding rules and guidance documents and are useful to be aware of as they influence on how apprenticeship programmes are delivered and documented:

- an apprentice must have the right to work in England and spend at least 50 per cent of their working hours in England

- the apprentice must be employed from the first day of their apprenticeship and have a contract of service with their employer, or an apprenticeship training agency (ATA)

- the apprenticeship must last for a minimum duration of 12 months, based on a 30-hour week, or an extended period for part-time apprentices

- at least 20 per cent of an apprentice's normal working hours, over the planned duration of the apprenticeship practical period, must be spent on OffTJ training

- an apprenticeship must include, where appropriate, progression towards, and attainment of, relevant approved English and maths qualifications

- the apprentice must complete an independent assessment at the end of their apprenticeship, known as an EPA.

TAKE IT FURTHER

To explore the current apprenticeship funding rules and what implications they may have for you, explore the government guidance at: www.gov.uk/guidance/apprenticeship-funding-rules. It may be helpful to consider the following:

- What are the responsibilities of employers and training providers when taking on new apprentices?

- What are the associated costs and benefits to those stakeholders involved with apprenticeship training?

- What impact should an apprenticeship programme have and how would this be demonstrated in an organisation?

- What would the similarities and differences be for a new employee undertaking an apprenticeship in a role they have never worked in before, and for an existing employee taking on a new role within an organisation and industry they have worked in for many years?

What is 'off-the-job' training?

As well as receiving training whilst at work to allow them to perform the duties they have been employed to do, today's apprentices also complete regular 'off-the-job' (OffTJ) training as part of their working hours. OffTJ training help apprentices to develop the new KSBs the need in order to meet the apprenticeship standard they are committed to achieving.

OffTJ training is different to on-the-job training, which an apprentice may need to carry out their role, particularly if they are new to the post and the industry. For example, a new apprentice may need their employer to train them in a number of key functions and processes so they can carry out their day-to-day role safely and effectively. However, these specific duties and competencies may not be included in the apprenticeship standard, designed by employers in the trailblazer group.

The Education and Skills Funding Agency (ESFA) and the government (Department for Education, 2019) have clear guidelines on what can be counted towards apprentice's minimum entitlement to OffTJ training equal to at least 20 per cent of their normal working hours:

- the teaching of theory – for example: lectures, role-playing, simulation exercises, online learning or manufacturer training;

- practical training – shadowing, mentoring, industry visits and participation in competitions;

- learning support and time spent writing assessments and assignments.

For example, an apprentice might spend one day a week away from their employer, studying theory and practical learning at a local college or training provider. Alternatively, they might travel to a national provider to undertake their OffJT training as part of a block placement, staying in local hotels or on-site residential accommodation. OffJT training could also take place at the apprentice's place of work, for example in a training room. As the minimum 20 per cent entitlement is over the duration of the apprenticeship, there are a wide range of different delivery and attendance models that different apprentices are likely to undertake, including training delivered online or through a blended learning approach.

FIND OUT MORE

The 'Taking Training Seriously' report, commissioned by the Gatsby Foundation (2018), compared OffTJ training as part of English apprenticeships to those in other countries. The report highlighted a number of key differences, for example the very diverse nature of English apprenticeships from a year-long Level 2 Groundworker apprenticeship, to the five-year Chartered Town Planner degree apprenticeship.

In many continental European countries, the report found clear distinctions in the different types of OffJT provided, such as general education, theoretical vocational education and practical training outside of their normal work. There were also significant differences in the amount of OffJT provided. The report highlighted that the current 20 per cent entitlement should be an absolute minimum, if England is to compete with the best apprenticeship programmes found internationally.

- Consider the eight key recommendations made in the report. To what extent do you agree with these recommendations in enhancing the quality and impact of apprenticeships?
- Exploring some of the international comparisons, which country's approach do you feel is most suitable in meeting the needs of today's apprentices and their employers? What is it about their approach that appeals to you most?

What is end-point assessment?

By the end of their apprenticeship programme, apprentices need to be able to demonstrate that they have achieved occupational competence by meeting the requirements of the apprenticeship standard. They do this by undertaking an end-point assessment (EPA) which is assessed independently by an end-point assessor.

Before an apprentice can attempt the EPA, they must have met all the requirements and mandatory aspects of the standard. These requirements could include the following:

- all on programme training has been completed and the apprentice has completed the minimum duration of the apprenticeship as defined in the standard, for example 12, 18 or even 60 months
- the achievement of English and mathematics qualifications, such as Functional Skills, where relevant
- a specific subject qualification if this is a requirement of the standard, for example
- the production of any evidence required to enable the apprentice to take part in the EPA, such as a professional evidence portfolio or showcase

- agreement and sign-off from the employer that the apprentice is working at, or above, the level of competency set out in the standard.

Once these requirements have been met, the apprentice has passed through the 'gateway' and is now eligible to undertake the independent EPA. The specific details and requirement of the assessment for each standard is contained in the relevant assessment plan. The assessment plan could look quite different for different standards but must include at least two different assessment methods from a range of possible options, such as the following:

- **test based:** for example, an online multiple-choice knowledge test, or a paper-based case study test taken under exam conditions

- **observation based:** for example, observing the apprentice carrying out different duties in their workplace.

- **discussion based:** such as an in-depth professional discussion or interview

- **presentation or project based:** for example, presentation of a portfolio 'showcase' of evidence.

The EPA will be carried out by an independent end-point assessor on behalf of an independent end-point assessment organisation (EPAO). These organisations must be approved and listed on the official EPAO register. The assessor must be suitably qualified and experienced in the occupational area and be impartial and independent from the training provider, employer or apprentice. This helps to ensure that the integrity of the assessment process is maintained and that employers can be confident that qualified apprentices really do have the minimum standards of competency required to carry out their occupation role.

EPAs are usually graded, for example pass, merit and distinction, or just pass and distinction. The assessment plan outlines the different grading criteria and any assessment weighting, for example competence demonstrated through an observation of practice might be more important in the assessment that a multiple-choice test, in demonstrating competence. The grading process helps to differentiate those apprentices who are able to meet the minimum standards and those learners who are working at a higher level of competence. If you were an employer, who would you rather employ for your business?

REFLECTION POINT

To what extent do you agree that achievement of a new apprenticeship will provide employers with a clear indicator of competence relating to a set national standard?

Do you feel that achievement of an apprenticeship standard will help apprentices to transfer jobs or move to a different employer or workplace, as they have a certificate which guarantees their capabilities?

If an apprentice is not able to demonstrate the minimum levels of competency to achieve a pass in their EPA, re-sits and re-takes will be available. A re-sit is simply another attempt at the EPA, usually within a specific time period, such as 3 or 6 months. However, an apprentice may need some additional learning and support in order to help them develop their competency and skills further, before undertaking a re-take.

Usually an EPA grade will be capped at a pass if the apprentice did not achieve on their first attempt. Therefore, teachers, trainers and employers really need to support, develop and prepare apprentices well before they reach the gateway and undertake their formal EPA. In the following chapters, we will explore how best to use different forms of initial and ongoing assessments, highly effective teaching and training methods, and useful support, feedback and guidance, to make sure that your apprentices are confident and successful.

Have a look at the following case study which explores the EPA requirements of the very popular level 3 Team Leader/Supervisor apprenticeship standard which was approved in 2016. The trailblazer group included employers from a wide range of businesses including Balfour Beatty, Barclays Bank, Boots, the BBC, the Civil Service, Sainsburys, Virgin Media and Gateshead Council.

CASE STUDY

Saad has just started a new job as a training consultant for a private training provider. He previously worked in retail and telecommunications, leading a regional team of store managers. Saad will be supporting a caseload of 35 apprentices on the level 3 Team Leader/Supervisor apprenticeship standard.

Saad's manager has asked him to explore the following assessment plan which highlights all the EPA requirements for this standard, which his apprentices must be able to demonstrate in order to achieve their certificate of achievement.

Minimum duration of apprenticeship:	12 months

Requirements to pass through the gateway:	• English and mathematics at level 2
	• confirmation from the employer that the apprentice is working at, or above, the level of occupational competence
	• completion of a portfolio of evidence, which could include the following:
	  • written accounts of activities that have been completed
	  • presentations and video/audio extracts
	  • project plans, reports and minutes of meetings
	  • observation reports
	  • feedback from managers, supervisors or peers
	  • continual professional development (CPD) log and personal development plan (PDP)
	  • performance reviews

(Continued)

(Continued)

End-point assessment method 1:	20-minute presentation with 30 minutes of questions and answers
End-point assessment method 2:	60-minute professional discussion supported by a portfolio of evidence
Order of assessment:	Any
Weighting:	Both assessment methods are weighted equally in their contribution to the overall EPA grade
Grades available:	fail, pass and distinction

REFLECTIVE QUESTIONS

- How could Saad ensure that he prepares his apprentices well to undertake their EPA for this standard?
- As a new training consultant, how could Saad develop his understanding of the different between a pass and a distinction grade achievement?

The diversity of new apprenticeships

There are around 600 different apprenticeship standards approved for delivery at different levels: intermediate (Level 2); Advanced (Level 3); Higher (Levels 4–7) and Degree (Level 6 and 7) in a wide range of vocational subject areas, including the following:

- Business, Administration and Law

- Construction, Planning and Engineering

- Education and Training

- Manufacturing and Logistics

- Arts, Media and Publishing

- Agriculture, Horticulture and Anima Care

- Health, Public Services and Care

- ICT

- Retail and Enterprise

- Leisure, Travel and Tourism

- Science and Mathematics

Unlike the previous SASE apprenticeship frameworks, employer-designed apprenticeship standards are specific to a given occupational role. This ensures that they support the learner to develop the specific KSBs that are required by their employer to carry out the role effectively. Of course, not all learners on each standard will be developing their skills from scratch. Different apprentices may well have quite different starting points, and these will need to be explored in detail, to ensure that learners are making progress and learning substantial new KSBs. It may also be the case that a learner is not quite ready to make a start on an apprenticeship programme, as they need further support and training to get ready for employment and further study. In these cases, a pre-apprenticeship programme might be a useful stepping stone between school and work, or to help a learner get back into employment after some time out of work. One possible route might be to complete a traineeship.

FIND OUT MORE

The Department of Education regularly publishes data on the number of apprentices starting programmes in England. The House of Commons briefing papers on apprenticeship statistics also provide a useful summary of the number of learners currently participating in an apprenticeship programmes, including breakdowns by age, level, gender, disability, ethnicity, region and employer size, as well as trends over time. The papers also highlight the most popular apprenticeship standards undertaken.

Find out more: www.apprenticeships.today/statistics

Traineeships

Introduced in 2013, traineeships are an education and training programme, with work experience. They are designed for those learners aged 16–24 who do not yet have the skills or experience needed to secure an apprenticeship or employment. Traineeships are usually unpaid and can last from 6 weeks up to 6 months, although most are completed in around 3 months.

Traineeships provide learners with work preparation training, such as developing a CV and improving their applied English and maths skills, along with a high-quality work placement of at least 100 hours, and a guaranteed interview at the end of the placement, to help the trainee progress.

Employers can work with a training provider to offer young people a work experience placement as part of their traineeship programme. The employer and training provider can agree on what the traineeship should include, the hours of work, the main duties to be undertaken by the learner, and the training provided by the employer as part of the placement. Traineeships can be in a wide variety of occupation areas, designed to help learners develop the skills and confidence needed to progress onto an apprenticeship, for example:

- Retail

- Business administration

- Warehousing

- Customer advisor

- Hairdressing

- Hospitality

CASE STUDY

Kieran left school four years ago having achieved only a couple of low-level formal qualifications. After claiming benefits for some time, he managed to find various short-term labouring jobs but nothing regular or long term. Kieran really wanted to work with cars. Some of his friends went on to complete their apprenticeship in vehicle maintenance, fitting and body repair after leaving school and are now in secure, full-time jobs. Kieran tried to apply for an apprenticeship after searching online; however, he was rejected three times due to a lack of any real work experience.

One of Kieran's friends suggested he speak to his local college. After a meeting with the Student Services team, staff found a motor mechanic traineeship lasting 7 weeks, with a local garage. The college helped Kieran to complete an online application, and following an interview with the garage manager, he was successful on gaining his traineeship.

Although unpaid, Kieran was able to develop a lot of new skills on his placement at the garage such as:

- Learning many aspects of motor vehicle maintenance, repair, and servicing of vehicles, including brakes, oil changes, exhausts, cambelts and radiators

- Booking in MOTs and services

- Assisting on vehicle recoveries following a breakdown

- General cleanliness and maintenance of the workshop

- Answering the phone and dealing with customer enquiries

- Ordering stock via online ordering system

As well as learning useful practical skills, the college also provided training and support for Kieran to work towards gaining formal qualifications in English and mathematics, as well as health and safety, and employability training.

Kieran had hoped that his traineeship work placement might give him the experience he needed to gain employment as an apprentice and to start a possible career in the automotive industry. He really enjoyed working as part of the team in the garage and the structure and routine to his working week. At the end of the placement, Kieran had proved his commitment to the role. He was delighted that his manager agreed to take him on as a paid motor vehicle service and maintenance technician apprentice. He really hopes this might lead onto a full-time role from there.

REFLECTIVE QUESTIONS

• What might prevent young people from taking a similar route to Kieran, to take the first steps on their learning journey to a new career?

• If you were involved with Kieran's traineeship, what might the learning programme look like? What skills and behaviours would need to be developed first to help him achieve his educational aspirations?

Qualification levels

For those new to teaching and training, it will be useful to understand the different qualification levels used across England, Wales and Northern Ireland, to see how different apprenticeship standards compare broadly with other qualifications at the same level. Table 1.1 shows the range of popular qualifications undertaken by students and how these compare and relate to the different levels of apprenticeship.

Table 1.1 Comparison of qualification levels

Level	Qualifications examples	Framework for higher education examples	Example apprenticeship standards
Entry	• Skills for Life at entry level • Entry level awards, certificates and diplomas • 'Foundation learning' pathways • Essential or Functional Skills at entry level		
1	• GCSEs graded 3-1 or D-G • NVQs at level 1 • Vocational awards, certificates and diplomas at level 1 • English for speakers of other languages (ESOL) at level 1 • 'Foundation learning' pathways • Essential or Functional Skills at level 1		
2	• **Level 2 (intermediate) apprenticeship** • CSE grade 1 • O level grade A-C • GCSEs graded 9-4 or A*-C		• Sport coach • Adult care worker • Equine groom

(Continued)

Table 1.1   (Continued)

Level	Qualifications examples	Framework for higher education examples	Example apprenticeship standards
	• NVQs at level 2 • Skills for Life • Vocational awards, certificates and diplomas at level 2, e.g. BTEC Tech Award, BTEC First • Essential or Functional Skills at level 2		• Apprentice barber • Childcare assistant
3	• Level 3 (advanced) apprenticeship • Access to higher education diploma • A levels • Advanced Extension Awards • International Baccalaureate • NVQs at level 3 • Applied general and tech level qualifications • Vocational awards, certificates and diplomas at level 3, e.g. BTEC/OCR nationals		• Hospitality supervisor • Retail team leader • Teaching assistant • Marketing and social media assistant • Learning mentor
4	• Level 4 (higher) apprenticeships • NVQs at level 4 • Higher National Certificates (HNC) • Vocational diplomas, certificates and awards	• Certificates of higher education (CertHE)	• Cyber security technologist • Software developer • Assessor/ coach
5	• Level 5 (higher) apprenticeships • Higher National Diplomas (HND) • Other higher diplomas • BTEC Professional Diplomas, Certificates and Awards • NVQ5	• Diplomas of higher education (DipHE) • Foundation degrees	• Learning and Skills Teacher • Clinical dental technician • Gold course manager
6	• Degree apprenticeships • Level 6 vocational professional diplomas, certificates and awards	• Bachelor degrees, graduate certificates and diplomas	• Probation officer • First officer pilot

(Continued)

Table 1.1 (Continued)

Level	Qualifications examples	Framework for higher education examples	Example apprenticeship standards
7	• Degree and integrated degree apprenticeships • Fellowships • Diploma in Translation • Advanced professional awards, certificates and diplomas	• Postgraduate certificates and diplomas, PGCE • Master's degree	• Clinical associate in psychology (CAP) • Senior journalist
8	• Level 8 specialist awards • Level 8 award, certificate and diplomas, e.g. strategic direction	• Doctorates (PhD, DPhil, Ed.D)	*apprenticeships are not funded at level 8*

(Adapted from 'What Qualification Levels Mean', www.gov.uk, 2020)

FIND OUT MORE

You can find each apprenticeship standard online at: www.instituteforapprenticeships.org/apprenticeship-standard

Each standard includes an occupation summary or profile, the key occupational duties of the role, and the specific KSBs required to meet the standard for that occupation role, as developed by the trailblazer employer group.

Explore a few examples of different apprenticeships standards that you are currently involved with, or may be in the future.

- To what extent does the standard meet your expectations?
- Do you agree with the key duties listed?
- Are the KBSs the ones that you would have listed as essential for today's apprentices to carry out the role effectively?
- Begin to think about the OffTJ training that apprentices would need in order to develop their KSB in line with the standard.

A vocational learning route

Traineeships and apprenticeships are a type of 'vocational learning', but what does this mean? Ingle (2020) highlights how vocational learning, often referred to as technical and vocational education and training (TVET), is often considered in contrast to the teaching of more traditional, 'academic' subjects and qualifications, such as English, maths and science, GCSEs and A levels. Vocational learning is often defined as the development of knowledge and behaviours linked to specific occupational skills, careers or job roles.

The Commission on Adult Vocational Teaching and Learning (CAVTL, 2013) suggests that vocational learning programmes must be characterised by two specific factors: a 'clear line of sight to work', which helps learners to see why, and what, they are learning is relevant in the real-world of work, and a 'two-way street' collaboration, between training providers and employers. Both traineeships and apprenticeships clearly meet these characteristics, as learners develop their knowledge and skills in an applied work context, with the support of their trainers, line managers and employers. This will hopefully be motivational for the apprentice, as they can see the impact of their learning quickly and how it helps them to be more effective at work.

Professor Martin Doel (cited in The Edge Foundation, 2019), Co-Director of the Centre for Post-14 Education and Work at the UCL Institute of Education (IOE), suggests that vocational education is defined by five key variables:

(1) What is taught – the content is drawn from the workplace whilst still respecting the need for rounded development in the student.

(2) Who is teaching – training from individuals with relevant vocational and industrial backgrounds.

(3) Where it is taught – in industry standard facilities.

(4) How it is taught – by practice-led learning.

(5) How it is assessed – by doing and practical demonstration, as well as by written examination.

It is clear to see that learners on apprenticeships don't just learn about abstract theories and ideas but also develop, and apply, the specific, work-related, practical and technical skills required in a particular occupation. This mix of development and progression through work, training and learning is very appealing to many learners at all ages, but particularly for many younger learners who are ready to 'earn while they learn' following their experiences at school.

REFLECTION POINT

For some people, vocational learning programmes are viewed as easier, less demanding options for less able learners, in contrast to more academic GCSEs and A-levels qualifications suited to more able learners who are progressing to higher education courses. The reality is, however, that many vocational learning programmes include significant, and demanding, academic content, along with opportunities for the developmental of applied practical and technical skills.

This lack of perceived parity is not common in many other countries, however, such as Germany, Switzerland and the Netherlands, where vocational and technical education is often regarded as high quality and high value and at least as demanding as academic qualifications, if not more demanding.

- Do you feel that vocational learning routes in the United Kingdom are considered as equal with other qualifications at the same level?
- Do you feel that the transition from frameworks to standards has helped to improve the image and status of apprenticeships?
- What more could be done to address this lack of parity if you believe it exists?

Key roles and organisations involved in the apprenticeship journey

We have already highlighted a number of key roles and different organisations involved in the design, delivery, assessment and quality assurance of the new apprenticeships. It is helpful to explore the different roles and organisations in a little more detail, as this can be a confusing area for practitioners new to apprenticeships.

Apprenticeship training providers, employer providers and support providers

An employer will usually work with an approved training provider to deliver apprenticeships for their staff and new apprentices. To receive government funds, training providers must be listed on the government's register of apprenticeship training providers, and commit to the principles of delivering a quality apprenticeship than meets the needs of employers and apprentices.

Providers include a wide range of different public, private and voluntary organisations such as:

- schools, colleges, universities and independent training providers

- football clubs, leisure centres, transport providers, nurseries and retail organisations

- councils, charities, NHS trusts and chambers of commerce

Larger employers, who pay the apprenticeship levy, can also choose to become an employer provider, training their own staff using the apprenticeship service to pay for the training. Employer providers also need to be listed on the approved register.

Examples of employer providers include:

- Metro Bank

- Her Majesty's Revenue and Customs (HMRC)

- London and South Eastern Railway

- Superdrug

- Royal Navy

- Leeds City Council

Organisations can also become a supporting provider who work as a subcontractor for a main or employer provider, to deliver apprenticeship training. In this case, the main or employer provider has responsibility for assuring the quality of all aspects of the apprenticeship.

ATAs recruit, employ and arrange training for apprentices on behalf of employers. They must be approved and listed on the government's register of approved ATAs. ATAs will recruit and support apprentices, placing them with a host employer who pays a fee in return for the apprentice's service. The ATA takes responsibility for payroll services, such as paying the apprentice's wages, tax, holiday and sick pay. If the host employer can no longer support the apprentice due to a change in their circumstances, the ATA will find alternative employment, so they can continue their apprenticeship.

Whatever the type of apprenticeship provider, staff will work closely with the apprentice and their employer throughout the learning journey. Let's take a look at the key people involved in the apprenticeship learning journey (Table 1.2).

Table 1.2 Key apprenticeship stakeholders

The apprentice	An apprentice must be over 16 and not in full-time education. There is no upper age limit. Apprentices need to be motivated to learn and work.
Vocational trainers	These are staff of providers, who develop the vocational and technical knowledge, skills and behaviours of their apprentices in a given occupation. They may be qualified teachers, lecturers and assessors, or working towards qualification. They will have relevant vocational experience and expertise, and should be able to motivate, inspire and develop their apprentices.
Coach or mentor	As well as vocational trainers, many apprentices also have a progress coach, training consultant or mentor, who guides and monitors their progress throughout their learning journey. The coach may complete regular progress reviews and tutorials with the apprentice. This role may also be carried out by the vocational trainer, or as a discreet role.
Specialist tutor	Where required, the apprentice may also need support and training to develop their applied English, mathematics and ICT skills. This may be carried out by a specialist skills teacher or trainer, or by the vocational trainer and/or coach depending on their skills, qualifications and the needs of the apprentice. If the apprentice has more specific learning needs, a specialist tutor may provide additional learning support where needed.
The employer	The employer is the organisation that employs the apprentice and pays them at least the national minimum wage for apprentices. Apprentices are also paid for their training, which represents at least 20 per cent of their working hours. The apprentice also needs the support of their day-to-day supervisor or line manager when progressing through their learning programme. The manager, coach and apprentice should all meet regularly to ensure that the apprentice is developing and progressing appropriately in their studies and in the workplace.

Let's explore how the different apprenticeship stakeholders work together in this case study of apprentice Kalpesh.

CASE STUDY

Kalpesh had always loved working with computers. He had enjoyed IT lessons at school and had even helped to build a few computers. He was always helping his family with technical problems, installing new software, and getting their devices connected to the internet.

After leaving school, Kalpesh had started to work in a supermarket stacking shelves and tidying the store, often working weekends and night shifts. He had impressed his manager and was a team leader. However, after a few years, Kalpesh was getting bored in the same role; it lacked the challenge he needed to stay motivated. He was also hoping to work during the day, keeping his evenings and weekends free so he could see his friends more often.

After searching different options online, Kalpesh applied for an Infrastructure Technician Apprenticeship at a local high school. They were looking for someone to install, maintain and repair software and hardware, troubleshoot faults, monitor the safe use of technology, catalogue resources even help develop the school website and virtual learning environment (VLE).

The school was his employer, and his line manager was the head of the IT network team, Louise, worked with an independent training provider to deliver the apprenticeship. Kalpesh attended OffTJ training in weeklong blocks every few months in Birmingham. The school paid for his travel and accommodation and he attended lessons at the training providers' offices in the city centre. His vocational tutors were really experienced and highly skilled. He always learned lots of new technical skills on his block placement which he could use back at school, for example installing new security software or completing hardware upgrades. He also took specialist technical exams in networking and operating systems.

Kalpesh also had a training coach called Marcus. Marcus visited the school every three months to carry out a review of his progress and to observe him carrying out different duties around the school. Kalpesh and Marcus would also speak regularly online using Microsoft Teams. He would get feedback from Marcus on his assignment work as he was building up his summative portfolio as part of his EPA. Marcus would also speak to Kalpesh's line manager Louise to identify challenging projects at school that he could complete as part of his EPA evidence.

REFLECTIVE QUESTIONS

*   What might prevent all the different stakeholders from working together effectively to support Kalpesh's learning journey?
*   If Louise was not available when Marcus carried out his progress reviews with Kalpesh, what should happen next to ensure that she is fully aware of Kalpesh's targets and priorities?

As well as the range of different stakeholders involved in the apprentice's journey, there are also a number of organisations that play a key role in the new apprenticeships.

Key organisations involved in the new apprenticeships

The Institute of Apprenticeships and Technical Education
(www.instituteforapprenticeships.org)

Created in 2017, and sponsored by the Department for Education, the Institute oversees the development, approval and publication of apprenticeship standards. They support the trailblazer groups of employers to develop, review and revise apprenticeship standards and assessment plans. They also oversee the delivery of external quality assurance (EQA) to ensure it is robust and carried out consistently across EQA providers. The IATE website includes links to all the current apprenticeship standards, including their assessment plans.

Education and Skills Funding Agency (ESFA)
(www.gov.uk/government/organisations/education-and-skills-funding-agency)

The ESFA is an executive agency for the Department of Education. The agency administers education funding for children, young people and adults, including the funding of apprenticeships for employers, employer providers and main training providers. The ESFA publishes detailed regulation and what can and cannot be funded as part of an apprenticeship, including specific conditions for dealing with subcontractors and supporting providers.

Each apprenticeship standard has a maximum funding band, which is the maximum contribution that the government will contribute towards the costs of delivering training and assessment for an apprenticeship standard. There are 30 different training bands that each standard fits into, ranging from £2,500, for an apprentice fire safety advisor, up to £27,000 for an apprentice watchmaker, boatbuilder or air traffic controller for example.

The Office of Qualifications and Examinations Regulation (Ofqual)
(www.gov.uk/government/organisations/ofqual)

Established in 2010 under the Apprenticeships, Skills, Children and Learning Act 2009, Ofqual regulates qualifications, examinations and assessments in England. This also includes EQA of all apprenticeship EPAs (except integrated degree apprenticeships) through the regulation of EPAOs.

Office for Students (OfS)
(www.officeforstudents.org.uk)

The OfS is the independent regulator of higher education in England. In a similar role to Ofqual, the OfS takes responsibility for the EQA of integrated degree apprenticeships through the regulation of EPAOs.

Office for Standards in Education (Ofsted)
(www.ofsted.gov.uk)

Ofsted is an independent organisation that reports directly to parliament. Their role is to make sure that organisations providing education and training in England do so to a high standard for students. As well as inspecting schools, Ofsted also inspects the quality of apprenticeship provision, carrying out inspections of independent training providers, local authorities and colleges. Ofsted also now inspects the quality of degree level apprentices, taking over the role once held by the OfS. We will explore the work of Ofsted in further detail in Chapter 6, including the expectations for the quality of education as laid out in the education inspection framework (EIF).

Federation of Awarding Bodies (FAB)
(www.fab.org.uk)

FAB is a trade association for vocational awarding bodies in the United Kingdom. They represent over 120 awarding bodies, providing information, advice and guidance to members and contributing to consultations by the government and the regulator. Many awarding bodies carry out the role of EPAO, for example Pearson, City and Guilds, TQUK and Active IQ.

University Vocational Awards Council (UVAC)
(www.uvac.ac.uk)

Established in 1999, UVAC is a not-for-profit membership organisation representing and supporting universities, colleges and other organisations with their implementation and delivery of higher and degree level apprenticeships.

Federation of Industry Sector Skills and Standards
(www.fisss.org)

The Federation is a charitable, membership organisation who works with government and employer run skills organisations to shape policy and practice around the UK skills system and workforce, including apprenticeship training. The Federation also provides online apprenticeship management systems and apprenticeship certification services.

FIND OUT MORE

The Federation of Industry Sector Skills and Standards represents a range of member-led partnerships including sector skills councils, sector skills bodies and national skills academies. Explore their member directory and find the member organisation who represents the apprenticeship occupations and standards that you work with: https://fisss.org/sector-skills-council-body/directory -of-sscs.

- How could these member organisations support your work in developing apprentice's KSBs in your sector?

End-point assessment organisations

As we briefly explored earlier, EPAOs arrange and conduct the process of independent EPA on behalf of employers and training organisations. They must have been assessed and approved and feature of the government's list of suitable EPAO organisations. EPAOs include a wide range of different organisations including:

- college or training providers

- assessment organisations

- awarding organisations

- higher education institutions

- professional and trade bodies

- sector skills councils, bodies and national skills academies

When an EPAO has confirmed that an apprentice has successfully passed their assessment, and relevant quality checks have been made, they can request a formal certificate on behalf of the apprentice through the apprenticeship assessment service.

FIND OUT MORE

Over 300 approved EPAOs, from a wide range of different organisations, are listed on the government's register of EPAOs, covering over 600 different apprenticeship standards.

Explore the current register and identify a few different EPAOs that carry out EPA for the standards that you are involved with.

- Which EPAO would you choose to work with as an employer or apprentice?
- What factors would influence your choice of EPAO?

REFLECTION POINT

Having explored the development of apprenticeships, what opportunities and challenges do the current format we see today offer to learners, trainers and employers?

Think about your own experience in the world of apprenticeships. Perhaps you are making the move straight from many years in the industry, or perhaps you are an experienced assessor on work-based learning courses or apprenticeships frameworks. What are the areas of development that are priorities for you?

Finally, think about any actions that you might set yourself as a result of reading this first chapter. Perhaps it might be helpful for you to explore a range of apprenticeship standards and their EPA assessment plans. You might want to use some of the support resources listed below to find out more about the structure and approach to today's new apprenticeships.

A summary of key points

In this chapter we have looked at a number of key themes:

- the development of apprenticeships over time and the move from apprenticeship frameworks to employer-designed standards

- a definition of vocational learning and how apprenticeships are focused on developing the KSBs required by today's employers

- the apprenticeship journey from the formation of a standard by the trailblazer group to the requirements of the EPA process

- the different stakeholders and key organisations involved with the design, delivery, support and assessment of the new apprenticeships

Key links

Government's apprenticeship service www.apprenticeships.gov.uk	Guidance for apprentices, employers and parents on what an apprenticeship is and a search facility to find current apprenticeship opportunities.
Online support for apprenticeship delivery from the Education and Training Foundation www.apprenticeships.today/ETF	The Education and Training Foundation is the expert body for professional development and standards in further education (FE) and training in England. They provide an excellent range of free resources to support the delivery and assessment of the new apprenticeships, including the apprenticeship provider toolkit and eLearning courses on end-point assessment and employer engagement.

━━ FURTHER READING ━━━━━━━━━━━━━━━━━━

Armitage, A. and Cogger, A. (2019) *The New Apprenticeships*. St. Albans: Critical Publishing.

Bradbury, A. and Wynne, V. (2020) *The Apprentice's Guide to End Point Assessment*. Los Angeles, CA: Learning Matters.

Department for Business, Innovation and Skills and Department for Education (2012) *Richard Review of Apprenticeships*. Available at: www.gov.uk/government/publications/the-richard-review-of-apprenticeships [Accessed: July 2020].

Department for Business, Innovation and Skills and Department for Education (2015) *Apprenticeships (in England): vision for 2020*. Available at: www.gov.uk/government/publications/apprenticeships-in-england-vision-for-2020 [Accessed: July 2020].

Department for Business, Innovation and Skills and Department for Education (2016) *Report of the Independent Panel on Technical Education*. Available at: www.gov.uk/government/publications/post-16-skills-plan-and-independent-report-on-technical-education [Accessed: July 2020].

Dixey, N. (2019) *Levy for Success*. Independently Published.

Field, S. and Windisch, H. (2016) *Building Skills for All: A Review of England: Policy Insights From the Survey of Adult Skills*. OECD. Available at: http://www.oecd.org/education/skills-beyond-school/building-skills-for-all-review-of-england.pdf [Accessed: July 2020].

2
PROGRAMME PLANNING

The basic idea behind teaching is to teach people what they need to know

Carl Rogers, humanistic psychologist

── IN THIS CHAPTER ──

In this chapter you will learn about:

* the importance of recruiting apprentices with integrity
* using initial assessments to establish apprentices' starting points and learning priorities
* planning and sequencing a programme of learning to ensure apprentices' development of substantial new knowledge, skills and behaviours

This chapter has the following links to the assessor-coach apprenticeship standard (level 4):

Skills: the Assessor-Coach will be able to:	Knowledge: the Assessor-Coach will understand:
S1 facilitate access to relevant, current information advice and guidance (IAG)	K1 sources of and how to access up-to-date and valid IAG
S2 apply or reference relevant initial and diagnostic assessment	K2 relevant forms of assessment to identify individual needs
S3 agree a programme of development and assessment, setting realistic but challenging goals that meet learners' and employers' needs	K3 how to agree individual programmes that inspire and challenge learners to achieve current work-related knowledge and skills
S4 liaise with employers, colleagues and others to support learners' development	K4 additional support for learners available through workplace and provider-based colleagues

Introduction

In Chapter 1 we explore the general requirements and components of the new apprenticeships. In this chapter, we are going to explore how we can design a programme of learning that really helps each apprentice to make progress towards their educational goals.

Respected psychologist Carl Rogers reminds us that the basic idea behind teaching is to teach people what they need to know, but what do your apprentices 'need to know'? To find this out, it is crucial to explore apprentices' starting points and to understand where they want to go, their next steps, their aspirations and ambitions.

It is important to recognise that an apprenticeship is not for everyone. Being able to 'earn while you learn' may be very appealing for many learners but this educational route can be incredibly demanding, especially where a learner is also juggling a busy private life, perhaps a busy family, working unsociable hours, taking care of loved ones.

As we explored in the last chapter, at least 20 per cent of an apprentice's contracted working hours need to be given over to training and learning. In reality, of course, it is likely that an apprentice will also need to commit more time to their educational journey to carry out research, to prepare for their assessments, to update their English and mathematics skills, for example. This requires commitment, motivation and often, a lot of hard work.

Employers may be very keen to use apprenticeship funding as a route to develop their staff, particularly if they are paying into the levy as a large employer. It may be tempting to see apprenticeship funding as a convenient way for staff to gain formal qualifications to recognise their existing skills and work experience.

However, the Education and Skills Funding Agency (ESFA) has strict funding requirements, and employers should ensure that they fully understand their employee's specific training needs, and level of prior learning, to ensure that the apprenticeship route is the most appropriate pathway. In the following case study, let's explore Oonagh's recent promotion and her specific training needs.

CASE STUDY

Since leaving school, Oonagh has worked for many years as a team member for a very large hospitality company. She enjoys her role working in a pub restaurant attached to a hotel owned by the same company. She mainly works on the early morning shift, greeting customers, introducing them to the breakfast buffet options and taking their orders for hot food. She waits on tables, serves the food, restocks the buffet and provides great customer service.

Oonagh is highly motivated and loves meeting new people. She is well respected by her colleagues and managers and has over ten years' service. When the shift supervisor is off sick or not available, Oonagh often steps up to complete their duties. She has been doing the job so long she finds the supervisor tasks easy and more interesting. She enjoys training new staff and taking on more responsibility.

A new food and beverage supervisor role was advertised and Oonagh was encouraged to apply. She was successful at the interview and her managers agreed that she has been carrying out the role informally for a while now. She has been invited to complete the level 3 hospitality supervisor

apprenticeship to gain a formal qualification in her new role. Oonagh left school with few qualifications and this would be a good way to recognise her skills and experience for her CV.

Oonagh has a meeting with her manager and a skills coach from the training provider. They explore
the knowledge, skills and behaviours of the apprenticeship standard and carry out an initial
assessment. Given Oonagh's experience, she is already very confident she has the large majority of
the KSBs required. Her manager agrees. She would need to learn more about budgeting and the
financial operations of the business, but she meets almost all the rest of the competency
standards. Oonagh is excited to get started - it won't take her very long to learn about the finance
aspects and she feels confident she will be able to take the end-point assessment and gain her
qualification in just a few months given her high levels of prior experience.

REFLECTIVE QUESTIONS

*   Is the apprenticeship route the right one for Oonagh, to ensure she has the knowledge and
    skills to be able to carry out her supervisor role?
*   What alternative training options might be more appropriate for Oonagh to undertake?

Whilst it would be useful for Oonagh to have formal qualification to recognise her expertise, the
minimum duration of the apprenticeship is 12 months. Given Oonagh's prior learning, it is clear that
she won't need this amount of training to close her knowledge gaps to meet the requirements of the
standard. Therefore, this apprenticeship route is not the right one to meet her needs and to fulfil the
funding requirements of the new apprenticeship.

Oonagh should not use apprenticeship funding simply to accredit her existing knowledge, skills and
behaviours. The training provider should advise her of this and signpost more appropriate alternatives,
such as professional short courses, or perhaps an alternative apprenticeship that might support her
progression to another role with her employer, such as a hospitality manager.

Recruiting with integrity

As we explored in chapter one, a new apprenticeship can be a really effective way for organisations to
help new staff develop the substantial new knowledge, skills and behaviours required for a specific
occupational role. The apprenticeship route may also be an effective way for an existing member of
staff to upskill or retrain, to develop the new skills and understanding required to carry out a role
within the same organisation, for example if they are taking on more managerial responsibilities.

Employers and training providers must ensure that the apprenticeship route is right for the individual
learner, and that it allows them to develop new skills, linked to their current job, that are different
to any qualifications they already hold. When apprentices are recruited with integrity in this way, it
can be an effective way of boosting their morale and motivation. It can also be a great way for the
organisation to show how much they value their staff, develop the skills required to keep their business
running effectively and encourage staff to stay with their employer.

Many organisations implement an apprenticeship application and recruitment process, which ensures that the route is best for the learner and the business. Employers may use one or more different training providers to offer apprenticeships in different areas and at different levels.

Providers and employers need to ensure that potential apprentices are provided with clear advice and guidance about what the apprenticeship route encompasses, the level of time and commitment they will need to make and the format and content of the end-point assessment. Employers, line managers and supervisors also need to be very clear about the expectations and requirements of the new apprenticeship route and how they will manage the off-the-job training requirements when their apprentice is released from their duties to complete their training. Employers also need to be realistic about the time needed for managers to meet regularly with the apprentice's training provider, so they can contribute fully to review meetings, shape the learning programme and help the apprentice undertake relevant work-related projects, tasks and activities that allow them to develop and progress.

If the apprenticeship is going to be a success, for all stakeholders, the importance of clear, realistic and transparent recruitment cannot be overstated. In line managers are not supportive, it will be very challenging for apprentices to have time away from their job to carry out their training in a meaningful way. If the apprentice is looking for a quick way to gain a qualification with minimal effort, they are likely to become bored and demotivated very quickly. If training providers enrol apprentices onto a specific standard with very high levels of prior learning and existing experience in that role, it is unlikely that they will need at least the minimum 12 month training time in order to develop the new knowledge, skills and behaviours required.

Establishing starting points

To ensure that an apprentice is on an appropriate programme of learning, the training provider, with the support of the learner and their employer, should undertake a process of initial assessment. This assessment can take many different forms but is essential to fully understand the apprentice's starting points. Where an apprentice has some existing prior learning, for example relevant work experience and achievement of previous qualifications, then this should be taken into account and the duration of the training adjusted accordingly.

By exploring apprentices' starting points, training providers can then plan an effective programme of learning that will fully meet their needs, and those of their employer. Establishing an accurate baseline of the apprentice's existing knowledge, skills and behaviours will help to ensure they are not receiving training for things they already know and can do. It is likely that the learning programme for an apprentice new to an organisation and job role will look significantly different to a more experienced member of staff who knows the business and vocational sector well, but is upskilling.

When the apprentice's starting point is fully established, a series of key targets, or milestones, can be set as part of the learning programme. This will help the training provider, employer and apprentice monitor progress over time and see the 'distance travelled' from the start of the apprenticeship, towards their end-point assessment, and ultimately the achievement of their key goals. In the following case study, we explore the different backgrounds and starting points of two learners who are considering an apprenticeship route.

CASE STUDY

Destiny and Nicole both want a career as a nurse. They have seen an opportunity to enrol on a level 5 nursing associate apprenticeship. Destiny left college having achieved a BTEC in Health and Social Care, along with Functional Skills qualifications in English and maths. She has been working in a local care home for the last four years, starting as a care assistant and progressing to a care manager. She is looking for a new challenge and would like to move into working with older patients in a hospital setting. Destiny is an excellent communicator, although she is dyslexic and can struggle with spelling. She has developed a range of good care skills, for example meeting her clients' needs for safety, dignity, privacy and comfort. She has undertaken many training courses whilst working at the home, for example in dementia care, infection control, safe handling of medicines and end-of-life care. Destiny would like to eventually become a qualified registered nurse in elderly care and sees this apprenticeship as a key stepping stone.

Nicole completed A levels in English, psychology and media studies at school and went on to complete a Higher National Diploma (HND) in marketing and public relations at university. She is an independent learner and has excellent study skills. After working in the communications department at a large hospital trust for the last five years, Nicole has decided on a change of career and would love to have a more rewarding role caring for patients as a nurse associate. Nicole was able to undertake some shadowing work at the hospital trust in different departments, to make sure the caring professions were right for her. After her work experience, she would really like to work in the urgent and emergency care department. Nicole is used to studying at level 5 but has no real clinical and care experience.

REFLECTIVE QUESTIONS

Think about the different starting points that Destiny and Nicole have.

- Do you think the nursing associate apprenticeship route is the right pathway for both Destiny and Nicole?
- How might a skills coach find out about Destiny and Nicole's prior experience and skills?
- How would their programme of learning be structured to reflect their different starting points?
- Give their different levels of experience, how would you challenge and support both learners on their apprenticeship journey?

Initial assessment

To carry a robust initial assessment, the training provider, apprentice and their line manager should work together to assess the learners' relevant work experience, prior education, training and qualifications against the knowledge, skills and behaviours listed in the apprenticeship standard. This three-way, or tripartite, process should identify the learner's baseline level of competency, identifying the remaining aspects of the standard which need to be learned. From this baseline, the apprentice's training programme can be designed (Figure 2.1).

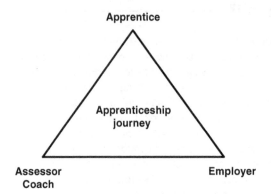

Figure 2.1 Tripartite planning process

The initial assessment process could be a professional discussion, which explores the learner's existing confidence and competency, their background and experience and any previously achieved qualifications if these are relevant to the apprenticeship standard. The use of initial assessment records will be helpful to review all the different KSBs listed in the apprenticeship standard. These are sometimes referred to as a 'skills scan'. Together, the assessor coach, apprentice and line manager can make a judgement of the level of existing prior learning (if any) and reflect this in the plan of learning. The role of the manager is particularly important when the apprentice is an existing member of staff who is upskilling or retraining. Even if the apprentice is new to the business, the line manager will be able to make a valuable contribution to the initial assessment process, for example explaining how a particular aspect of the KSBs applies to the occupation role in practice, or to ask the learner relevant questions to unpick any prior learning.

A relevant scale could be used to agree on the current level of competency and skill each learner has, which will be helpful to identify specific priorities for training. However, care should be taken to ensure that the process of initial assessment does not reply on a simple 'skills scan' of the apprentice's own judgement alone. It can be very difficult to self-assess one's own level of competence accurately. Apprentices may not know what they don't know, or they may lack confidence and underestimate what they know and can already do. Therefore, the tripartite discussion between a suitably experienced skills coach or training consultant, a relevant manager or supervisor, and the apprentice, will allow an accurate baseline judgement to be agreed.

Let's explore the following case study where Stuart is wondering how to improve the initial assessment process used at a training provider.

CASE STUDY

Stuart works as an apprenticeship delivery manager for a further education college. He manages a team of 12 skills coaches. Stuart has worked with apprenticeships for over ten years, previously on the frameworks and now on the new apprenticeship standards. His team of coaches each has a caseload of apprentices on different standards including business administration, team leader and retailer.

A number of apprentices have been leaving their learning programme early or have taken much longer than expected to successfully move through the gateway to end-point assessment. Stuart has decided that improvements need to be made to the initial assessment process. He feels the existing skills scans are too simplistic. Apprentices often complete these very quickly and there is little input from their employers or managers.

Starting with the level 2 retailer apprenticeship standard, Stuart has developed four different initial assessment tools to try and measure apprentice's starting points more effectively. He hopes this may help his team of coaches to plan a learning programme which meets the needs of apprentices and their employers much better.

KSB Brand reputation	0-24 Don't know/can't do this	25-49 I have some basic awareness/ skills	50-74 I am quite confident in this area most of the time	75-100 I am fully confident in this area - no development needs	**Your score:**
Respond to situations that threaten brand and business reputation in line with company policy and alert the relevant person if a threat is identified					
KSB Brand reputation	1 I have no/ minimal knowledge or skills in this area	2 I have some of the knowledge and skills needed in this area to carry out my role but I am not fully confident	3 I have some of the knowledge and skills needed in this area to carry out my role but I do not use them consistently with full confidence	4 I can demons-trate full competence consistency in this area while carrying out my role	**Priority need: Red/ Amber/ Green**
Respond to situations that threaten brand and business reputation in line with company policy					

(Continued)

(Continued)

and alert the relevant person if a threat is identified					
KSB Brand reputation	Emerging (just starting)	Developing (showing an increased competence)	Secure (meeting competence expectations most of the time)	Mastered (demonstrating full competence consistently)	**Rationale for grade**
Respond to situations that threaten brand and business reputation in line with company policy and alert the relevant person if a threat is identified					
KSB Brand reputation	This does not describe me at all	This describes me sometimes in my role	This is a fair description of me carrying out my duties	This is an exact description of me and what I do in my role	**Evidence to support judgement**
Respond to situations that threaten brand and business reputation in line with company policy and alert the relevant person if a threat is identified					

REFLECTIVE QUESTIONS

- Which of the four different assessment rubrics do you think apprentices would find the easiest to complete accurately and why?
- What additional changes would you make to improve the assessment tool further?
- Why might allocating a number, colour or grade to each judgement be useful throughout the apprenticeship journey?

- What is the value of asking for a rationale and evidence to support a particular judgement?
- Should the judgement be based on the apprentice's view only, or that also of their line manager and coach?
- If you were the skills coach, what would you do differently for an apprentice rating themselves with no skills, and another highlighting high levels of confidence and competence?

Initial assessment records, skills scans and competence diagnostic tools are only as useful as the validity and reliability of the information provided. Apprentices need to be able to fully understand what each knowledge, skill or behaviour statement means, in order to make an informed judgement on their current level of competency. The training provider, and line manager, can also help the apprentice with the initial assessment process by asking relevant questions and probing more deeply into their prior learning and experience, and current role and responsibilities, if applicable.

It is always helpful to consider a relevant rationale, and supporting evidence, to justify the assessment judgement to ensure the accuracy of the benchmarking process. For example, a new apprentice may *feel* that they are already very confident in a particular knowledge or skill area, but their manager may understand much better the limitations of their current competency, helping to assess their starting points, and training needs, much more accurately.

The apprenticeship EPA assessment plan, and sometimes an additional occupational brief provided with some standards can also provide more valuable information on the level of competency expected for this particular skill. For example, what do apprentices need to know and do to achieve a distinction in each component? With this information, the apprentice may well initially assess their skills differently. This is important, to allow the training provider and employer to plan the on- and off-the-job training and support required to allow the apprentice to develop and make significant progress.

Some standards also include a mandatory requirement to achieve specific qualifications in order for the apprentice to demonstrate their competence and undertake end-point assessment. These could include qualifications in information and communication technology (ICT), safeguarding children and vulnerable adults, or professional, vendor qualifications in project management or specific IT software, for example. Where these requirements form part of the apprenticeship standard requirement, the apprentice's starting points in these areas should also be thoroughly investigated and assessed.

TAKE IT FURTHER

Explore the KSBs, the EPA assessment plan guidance and any additional occupational brief (if applicable) for a standard you are working with. How would you structure an initial assessment discussion to accurately establish your apprentice's baseline? Think about what you will do next to structure a programme of learning which builds on this baseline starting point and helps them to develop the substantial new knowledge and skills they require to make progress in the workplace.

English and maths

As we explored in chapter one, the requirements of apprentices also include the achievement of approved qualifications in English and maths where these have not already been achieved, for example a GCSE pass at grade 4 (previously grade c) or higher, or an alternative qualification on the approved list, for example Functional Skills. For learners undertaking an apprenticeship at level 3 or above, they should hold or achieve approved level 2 qualifications in both English and maths before they can successfully complete. For learners undertaking a level 2 apprenticeship, they will need to have achieved English and maths at level 1, and work towards taking the tests in both subjects prior to undertaking their end-point assessment. They usually do not need to pass the test for level 2, however, unless this is specifically standard in the assessment plan for a specific standard.

As part of the initial assessment process, training providers, employers and the apprentice themselves should be aware of the learner's level of proficiency in these mandatory skills. This will be important in helping them to further develop their applied English and mathematics skills whilst progressing in their job role and on their apprenticeship. Even where an apprentice has already achieved the minimum level of qualification required, their current level of proficiency with applied English and maths should still be assessed and understood, as it may have been some time since they studied these subjects and completed their qualifications.

Undoubtedly, the need for all apprentices to have an effective level of functional English and maths skills, in both their personal and professional lives, should not be underestimated. Developing the literacies needed for learning, the skills to complete basic calculations, the ability to write a fluent report or email, the knowledge to allow them to accurately use punctuation are all identified by employers as key skills needed by their workforce. They could mean the difference between getting that job or being rejected for promotion.

Convincing some apprentices of the importance of these skills may not be an easy task, however. Many apprentices may have a history of low success in both English and mathematics from school or college. They may have a very low self-concept, or belief, about their ability to make any real progress in these subjects. Indeed, many apprentices may be of the impression that they left these lessons behind when they left school. Why do they need to learn maths now?

'I'm no good at maths', 'we're not very mathematical in our family' or 'my spelling is shocking' are phrases often heard by many Functional Skills tutors when they first meet an apprentice. The need to identify learner's starting points in English and maths is a key area to explore at the start of any apprenticeship, to identify the gaps and to put together a programme of learning that will help to close these gaps, improve confidence and prepare apprentices for any formal assessments that may be required. This could be a role for a specific English and maths coach or tutor, who supports apprentices as part of a group or individually. The vocational trainer may also take on this role if they have appropriate English and mathematics skills themselves.

Getting the 'IDEAS'

Many training providers make use of sophisticated, and sometimes very expensive, initial assessment and diagnostic software programmes to help identify learner's starting points. These programmes often react to the learner's responses as they get questions right, or wrong, producing a report that suggests an overall level of current ability. More detailed diagnostic programmes often produce an individual report of the learner's specific skills strengths and gaps. Trainers and coaches can then direct and signpost learners to specific resources and training session which may be helpful.

Providers may follow a five-stage **'IDEAS'** process to initially assess, diagnose, explore, advise and support learners' skills needs and knowledge gaps (Figure 2.2).

Again, as with any assessment, the outcomes are only as valid and reliable as the information inputted. Many diagnostic assessments can take over 40 minutes to complete. If the apprentice is not focused and committed to complete these appropriately and accurately, the results may not represent a realistic picture of their current skills and knowledge gaps. This may lead to an ineffective programme of learning and support.

Whilst online, automated assessments may be very efficient when working with large numbers of apprentices, alternative and complementary initial assessment methods may also be suitable, or even more effective at understanding your learner's starting points. For example, having a detailed conversation with an apprentice can often give you vital information about their prior learning and education challenges. Asking your apprentice to handwrite a paragraph of text on a subject of their choice can often highlight a specific area for development such as being able to accurately structure a sentence or paragraph, spelling issues, using punctuation and grammar appropriately. You might consider using a 'free-writing analysis' to explore any obvious needs at the start of their programme.

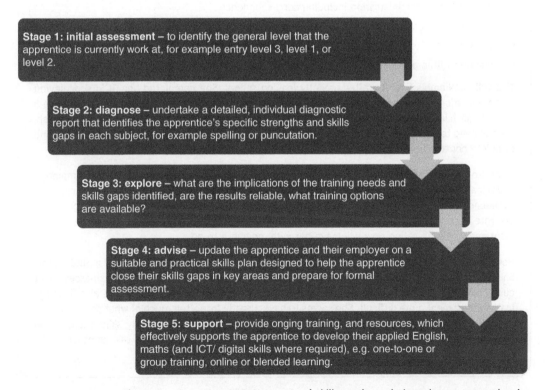

Stage 1: initial assessment – to identify the general level that the apprentice is currently work at, for example entry level 3, level 1, or level 2.

Stage 2: diagnose – undertake a detailed, individual diagnostic report that identifies the apprentice's specific strengths and skills gaps in each subject, for example spelling or puncutation.

Stage 3: explore – what are the implications of the training needs and skills gaps identified, are the results reliable, what training options are available?

Stage 4: advise – update the apprentice and their employer on a suitable and practical skills plan designed to help the apprentice close their skills gaps in key areas and prepare for formal assessment.

Stage 5: support – provide onging training, and resources, which effectively supports the apprentice to develop their applied English, maths (and ICT/ digital skills where required), e.g. one-to-one or group training, online or blended learning.

Figure 2.2 Four stage 'IDEAS' process of skills needs analysis and programme planning

FIND OUT MORE

The government publish the subject content for current Functional Skills qualifications in English and mathematics. Reformed Functional Skills qualifications, launched in September 2019, are aligned to these standards at the different levels. These documents provide useful guidance to all apprenticeship tutors and coaches who are supporting apprentices to develop their applied English and mathematics skills.

Explore the subject content at: www.apprenticeships.today/FS-English and www.apprenticeships .today/FS-maths

In the following case study, we meet Niamh who has been asked to complete a number of initial assessments by her training provider.

CASE STUDY

Niamh is excited to start her new level 3 apprenticeship in business administration for a local estate agent. Her main duties will include the following:

- general office administration including correspondence
- handling customer queries and liaising with service providers
- answering the telephone, online chat, emails and social media communications
- working within a small team to update customer management systems.

This will be Niamh's first job after recently leaving school. She completed her GCSEs, achieving grade 6 in information technology, grade 5 in art and design, grade 4 in mathematics and grade 3 in her English language and literature exams. As she has not achieved at least a grade 4 in English, she will need to complete her level 2 Functional Skills in English in order to undertake her EPA and complete her apprenticeship.

As part of her apprenticeship enrolment and induction, Niamh's skills coach asks her to complete a skills scan. Her coach says this is really for audit purposes and she should probably rate her confidence with each of the areas as quite low, as she is only at the start of the programme. She can rate herself with a higher score later on, which will demonstrate progress for her end-point assessment. A high rating now will leave her with, nowhere to go,

Her coach also provides a login for an online diagnostic assessment for both English and maths. She is asked to complete these in advance before the meeting. Niamh finds the English assessment quite challenging, but she takes her time and answers all the required questions. She also finds the maths assessment quite difficult. She seems to have already forgotten much of what she learned in her school maths lessons! As she already has her grade 4 GCSE, she quickly skips through the questions, getting some right and many wrong. She knows she won't have to take another maths exam.

At the meeting with her skills coach, she reviews the diagnostic reports. The English report highlights a number of strengths, such as being able to identify implicit and inferred meaning in texts and using textual features and devices. The report also highlights several areas for development, such as spelling and using punctuation markers accurately, such as colons, inverted commas, apostrophes and quotation marks. This is no real surprise to Niamh; she's always struggled in these areas even with the support of her school teachers. Her skills coach records her results and tells her to use the online resources portal where she will find activities and worksheets to develop these skills, in preparation for her Functional Skills exam.

Niamh and her coach also review her maths results, which suggest she is working at level 1, even though she has a grade 4 at GCSE level. Her coach tells her this doesn't really matter as she is exempt from having to do Functional Skills in maths. If she wants to brush up on her maths, she can always use the online resources, but she doesn't have to.

REFLECTIVE QUESTIONS

- How reliable are the skills scan, the initial assessment and diagnostic results? Do they really establish Niamh starting points to plan a programme of learning that will help her to progress?

- What are the advantages and disadvantages of using online software for establishing apprentice's existing skills in English and maths?

- Do you think that the online learning resources will be effective in developing Niamh's skills gaps and preparing her for the upcoming examination in English?

- If you were the skills coach working with Niamh, what plan for learning and support would you suggest for English and maths as part of her apprenticeship?

Additional learning and support needs

As well as exploring your apprentice's prior learning and qualifications, relevant work experience and current levels of competence with English, maths and where relevant ICT, another essential aspect of the initial assessment process is to explore any additional and specific learning and support needs. These needs could include any learning difficulties and differences, such as special educational needs and disabilities (SEND), neurological and specific learning differences (SpLDs) and any additional learning support (ALS) which may be required. Some learners up to the age of 25 with more complex needs may have an education, health and care plan (EHCP), which sets out their additional needs. Table 2.1 explores some of the more common SpLDs.

An apprentice may have a broad range of learning and pastoral needs, ranging from low confidence and self-esteem, mental health issues or financial difficulties. Learners' needs will need to be taken into account by training providers and employers at the start of an apprenticeship, to ensure that the learning programme makes any reasonable adjustments needed. Additional learning support may be

Table 2.1 *Some of the more common specific learning differences and difficulties*

Dyslexia	Around 1 in 10 of the population is thought to be dyslexic. Learners may demonstrate some difficulties with reading and spelling, remembering and processing information.
Dyscalculia	Estimates suggest around 3–6 per cent of the population may be affected by dyscalculia. Learners have difficulties with numbers, counting and performing calculations.
Dysgraphia	Learners have difficulties with handwriting, writing legibly and fluently.
Dyspraxia	Sometimes known as developmental coordination disorder (DCD), this SpLD is through to affect around 5 per cent of the population. Learners may have some difficulties with physical co-ordination, special awareness, balance and completing some practical tasks.
Attention deficit disorder (ADD)/ attention deficit (hyperactivity) disorder (ADHD)	Estimates suggest around 4 per cent of children may have ADHD. Learners may have difficulties with concentrating, organisation and staying focused. They may be easily distracted, often changing activity or task.
Autism spectrum condition (ASC)	A lifelong developmental disability, around 1 in 100 people are thought to have ASC. Learners may have difficulties with communicating, socialising and interacting with other people.

provided on a one-to-one basis by specialist tutors who have received appropriate training. Alternatively, some needs may be met through a range of different approaches, such as:

• extra guidance and support provided by the vocational tutor or skills coach

• additional time provided to complete assignment work or learning modules

• use of alternative assessment methods, such as professional discussion, verbal presentations or question and answer sessions

• more frequent progress reviews to monitor distance travelled

• allocation of a learning mentor to help develop study skills or support social and emotional needs

• closer monitoring by the manager, supervisor or workplace buddy

• specific information, advice and guidance provided by student support colleagues.

Learning support funding is available for training providers to meet the costs of putting in place reasonable adjustments for apprentices with a learning difficulty or disability where this affects their ability to continue and complete their apprenticeship.

TAKE IT FURTHER

Funded by the Department for Education, the 'Teaching for Neurodiversity - A Guide to Specific Learning Difficulties' (www.apprenticeships.today/learning-differences) provides a useful summary of some of the most common SpLDs, what challenges learners may face in their learning and education and useful sources of further information.

- Explore the guide and think about how you might best support an apprentice with an SpLD.
- What could you do in your role and where would you need to get further specialist guidance and support to meet their learning needs?

Training providers, coaches, learning mentors, tutors and employers should all be mindful of other challenges and barriers to learning that apprentices may face right from the start, and throughout their apprenticeship, such as problems at work, redundancy, financial hardship, substance misuse and mental health problems. Many larger providers may have specific learner support departments, counselling services and discretionary funds to help learners with specific difficulties, to try and keep them on track for achievement. These support mechanisms should be considered in the planning of the apprenticeship learning programme, if they are identified from the outset, and will hopefully support the learner to make good progress and complete their studies.

FIND OUT MORE

The 'Access to Work Mental Health Support Service' provides apprentices with support from a team of specialist advisors who can offer workplace support, coping strategies, a well-being support plan and workplace adjustments, designed to help any apprentice with a mental health condition.

Find out more: www.apprenticeships.today/health-support

Making the commitment

When apprentices have been recruited and are ready to start their learning programme, the employer and the apprentice must agree and sign an apprenticeship agreement which identifies:

- the specific apprenticeship standard connected to the apprenticeship

- the dates during which the apprenticeship is expected to take place

- the amount of off-the-job training that the apprentice is to receive.

The training provider must then agree and complete a commitment statement, with the employer and apprentice. This agreement confirms that all the requirements of funding are in place and that the employer has agreed the apprenticeship route is the most appropriate for the learner. The employer also needs to formally agree to allow the apprentice to complete their off-the-job training entitlement during their normal working hours and provide them with appropriate support and supervision.

This commitment is essential if the apprentice is to really develop substantial new knowledge, skills and behaviours whilst on the programme. Training providers should remind employers of this commitment they made at the start of an apprenticeship, if the learner struggles to be released from their duties to attend training and review session further down the line. This can be difficult when the employer is particularly busy or short-staffed. The format and frequency of the off-the-job training should be clearly negotiated and mapped out in advance to ensure this time is protected from the start and throughout what could be many months, or years, of study.

CASE STUDY

Apprentices may complete their off-the-job training through a wide range of different approaches, but all require effective planning and a firm commitment from the employer, to ensure the apprentice receives their minimum entitlement. For example:

- Adam is released from work for one day each week to attend his training as part of a group with other learners at his local FE college. He enjoys being away from the office and likes to use the library to carry out research and complete his assignment work between lessons.

- Claire undertakes her training through evening classes, as this is the only time her professional training is delivered. Although this time is outside her normal working hours, her employer provides the time back in lieu each week, and she finishes early on a Friday.

- Simon undertakes training at his employer's premises, as he often needs to use specific equipment and resources. Although he is still at work, he is completing training away from his usual day-to-day duties on the shop floor.

- Kunaal travels to his training provider's premises, which includes access to very specialist indoor and outdoor equipment, training rooms and learner support facilities. He undertakes a three-week block of off-the-job training, staying in local accommodation. These blocks are scheduled away from peak times of year when his company are especially busy and it would be difficult to release staff.

- Paul completes his off-the-job training using an online learning platform. He watches videos, participates in discussion boards and completes quizzes at quieter times when he is at work. Each week, he books a training room at work to attend a live lecture with his tutor and other apprentices around the country.

As well as the employer's commitments, the training provider also commits to planning and delivering a high-quality apprenticeship for their learners. The commitment statement should include an outline plan of training, recording learner's starting points and providing a road map to achievement. The plan should include the following:

- any prior learning relevant to the standard undertaken, for example work experience, prior education, training or qualifications in a related sector subject area

- the outcomes of English and maths assessments and the support to be provided, including the time to study for formal qualifications if required

- the outcomes of any learning support assessment and the support to be provided if necessary

- details of the specific training provided to develop the apprentice's occupational competence, for example lessons, lectures, modules, webinars and online learning

- any additional training components, qualifications and assessments that the apprentice may complete as part of their apprenticeship, to develop the skills and behaviours that allow them to make a positive contribution in their workplace

- arrangements for the employer, training provider and apprentice to meet regularly to formally review and assess the apprentice's progress on their programme

- any key milestones for the achievement of specific learning components, leading up to the gateway assessment.

Closing the gap

Now that the apprentice's starting points are fully understood, the 'gap' between where the apprentice currently is, and where they need to get to, becomes clear. The next step is to design an engaging programme of on- and off-the-job training and work experience that closes this gap between current knowledge, skills and behaviours, and the expected standard of occupational competency. This is the minimum distance that the apprentice will need to travel if they are to be successful in their independent end-point assessment (Figure 2.3).

Figure 2.3 'Mind the Gap' – using initial assessment to identify the specific knowledge, skills and behaviours that an apprentice needs to develop

Hopefully, many apprentices will exceed this minimum standard, developing deep knowledge and highly effective vocational skills and professional workplace behaviours that will help them to achieve their educational goals and career aspirations.

So how should training providers, and employers, plan a programme of effective training to help the apprentice close the gap? A 'one size fits all' approach is unlikely to help individual apprentices make sustained and substantial progress from their starting points. Vocational trainers, coaches, learning mentors and employers need to devise and develop an appropriately structured and sequenced framework of training, a curriculum, that allows individual apprentices to develop the technical knowledge, practical skills and confidence they need to progress in their role.

For example, some apprentices may need to prioritise the learning of key health, safety and security aspects of their vocational area and work role at the very start of their apprenticeship, before they can safely start to explore other aspects of learning. Apprentices new to an occupational role may well need to focus on developing the fundamental building blocks of new knowledge, learning key facts and procedures to develop a secure understanding of the 'basics', before being able to progress to more complex, abstract, conceptual learning. Some apprentices may need to focus on developing the study skills and confidence needed to learn independently and to make the best use of their time between off-the-job learning sessions. Other apprentices may need to be challenged with very specific, more complex learning that meets the needs of their employers, extending their baseline knowledge further.

Therefore, learning programmes and training plans could look quite different for different apprentices, as their starting points may also be very different. Remember Destiny and Nicole from our earlier case study? Both have just started on their nursing associate apprenticeship but have very different starting points. Destiny has four years' experience working in a local care home as a care assistant and care manager. She has already developed a range of good care skills and knowledge of dementia care, infection control, safe handling of medicines and end-of-life care. Nicole, on the other hand, has developed independent study skills and is used to working at level 5 but has no real clinical and care experience.

REFLECTION POINT

- How might the programme of learning be structured and sequenced differently for both Destiny and Nicole given their different skills and experiences?
- What priorities would their skills coach have when supporting each of them through their apprenticeship journey?
- What would the impact be if both apprentices took identical programmes in terms of formal training, work experience and placements, target setting and individual support?

FIND OUT MORE

The Ofsted education inspection framework (EIF) highlights the importance of carefully developing an appropriately sequenced and planned curriculum so that new knowledge and skills build on what learners already know and can do. This helps apprentices to progress and develop incrementally from their starting points, so over time, they know more and can do more.

- *Leaders, managers and teachers have planned and sequenced the curriculum so that learners can build on previous teaching and learning and develop the new knowledge and skills they need.*
- *The curriculum intent takes into account the needs of learners, employers and the local, regional and national economy, as necessary.*

Explore the education inspection framework and what makes the quality of education 'good' and 'outstanding'.

A summary of key points

In this chapter we have looked at a number of key themes:

- the need to recruit apprentices with integrity, to ensure the apprenticeship route is the most appropriate to meet their career goals and aspirations and the needs of their employer

- the importance of using effective initial assessments to accurately identify apprentices' starting points, training priorities and learning needs

- how training providers and employers need to plan and sequence an appropriate programme of learning to ensure that all apprentices develop the substantial new knowledge, skills and behaviours required to meet, and exceed, occupational competence.

Key links

British Dyslexia Association www.bdadyslexia.org.uk/advice/educators	Resources and guidance for educators on supporting learners who are dyslexic, or have another SpLD.
Patoss (Professional association of teachers of students with specific learning difficulties) www.patoss-dyslexia.org	Guidance, information and resources for teachers of students with specific learning differences and difficulties.
Apprenticeship commitment statement www.gov.uk/government/publications/ apprenticeship-commitment-statement- template	A template for the commitment statement employers must sign with their apprentice and training provider before training can start.

■■ FURTHER READING

Department for Education (2019) *Apprenticeship Off-the-Job Training: Policy Background and Examples*. Available at: www.gov.uk/government/publications/apprenticeships-off-the-job-training [Accessed: July 2020].

Education and Skills Funding Agency (2019) *Apprenticeships: Initial Assessment to Recognise Prior Learning*. Available at: www.gov.uk/government/publications/apprenticeships-recognition-of-prior-learning/apprenticeships-initial-assessment-to-recognise-prior-learning [Accessed: July 2020].

Greer, I. (2019) *The Vocational Assessor Handbook*, 7th ed. London: Kogan Page.

3
EFFECTIVE APPRENTICESHIP TEACHING AND TRAINING

The mind is not a vessel to be filled, but a fire to be kindled.

Plutarch of Chaeronea, philosopher

—— IN THIS CHAPTER ——

In this chapter you will learn about:

- different theories of training, instruction and learning to guide your approach
- using evidence-based teaching methods, strategies and approaches to maximise impact
- the importance of educators and employers working together to deliver training
- pitching the level of learning just right for optimal performance
- practical tips for using technology-enhanced learning (TEL) in your toolkit

This chapter has the following links to the assessor-coach apprenticeship standard (level 4):

Skills: the assessor-coach will be able to:	Knowledge: the assessor-coach will understand:
S5 anticipate and overcome barriers to progress and inspire achievement, ensuring that learning is inclusive and supports diversity	K5 strategies for inspiring learners, increasing their resilience in overcoming barriers and obstacles, and in raising concerns

(Continued)

(Continued)

Skills: the assessor-coach will be able to:	Knowledge: the assessor-coach will understand:
S6 highlight learners' mathematics and English needs, and signposts to appropriate support	K6 maths and English underpinning vocational skills and how to access additional support
S7 give timely feedback on progress towards mastery of relevant skills and knowledge	K7 effective practice in giving feedback to guide progress and achievement
S9 promote the safe and effective use of digital and mobile technologies to support learners and the assessor-coach role	K9 current and emerging technologies that could safely and effectively support learner autonomy and the assessor-coach role

Introduction

The opening quote from philosopher Plutarch encourages us to consider our roles as educators, trainers and teachers on apprenticeship programmes. Is our role to present, communicate and 'transmit' new information and material to those less experienced, knowledgeable and competent? Or is our role more one of facilitator, to inspire and challenge our apprentices to think hard and construct their own meaning and understanding? Arguably, the role of the modern apprenticeship tutor is both. Apprentices will need the instruction, guidance and expertise of experienced vocational tutors and trainers to provide them with the solid foundation of essential knowledge and skills they need to progress and survive in the workplace. Over time, apprentices will need to use and apply this foundation in their own place of work, taking on new challenges, using their initiative and developing their independence as they are challenged to develop their own skills and expertise. Apprenticeship educators will need to facilitate a blend of high-quality on- and off-the-job training which meets the individual needs of apprentices, so they become more knowledgeable, skilled, independent, creative, resourceful, inquiring, respectful and ultimately successful, individuals, employees and members of society.

The new apprenticeship programme is primarily designed to develop learners' knowledge, skills and behaviours to meet a level of occupational competency. However, much more than just a route to assessment and accreditation, a new apprenticeship is also a programme of education, training and development that should aim to personally develop the whole individual. This chapter explores practical ways that vocational trainers, skills coaches, instructors, learning mentors and employers can help apprentices to develop holistically, to become confident and occupationally competent in their apprenticeship standard.

Training or education?

Is the aim of a new apprenticeship to 'train' or to 'educate' the apprentice, or both? Ingle and Duckworth (2013a) identify that training is often seen as preparing learners to have the *procedural knowledge*, or 'know-how', in order to become competent in a particular skill or procedure. Education, however, is sometimes viewed as developing an understanding of more theoretical or abstract concepts, often referred to as declarative or *propositional knowledge*, or the 'knowing-of'.

As we explored in Chapter 1, the previous apprenticeship frameworks were often criticised for being a collection of different competency qualifications completed at different points throughout a programme of learning. This collection of components, mainly driven by training providers rather than employers, often had a significant focus on the assessment of existing skills, and the completion of evidence records required to meet awarding organisation requirements. Many apprentices were allocated an assessor, to help them achieve their qualifications, a descriptor which arguably reinforces the focus of the 'assessment model' of the older style apprenticeships.

The structure and format of the new employed-designed apprenticeship standards do much to move away from the limitations of the previous model. The role of assessor has been enhanced and expanded to one of 'training consultant' or 'skills coach', which helps to signal a distinct shift in the main purpose of the role, to one of teacher, instructor and trainer. This 'new breed' of education professional plays a key role, along with the apprentice's manager, supervisor, mentor and colleagues, in supporting apprentices to develop substantial new knowledge, along with the practical technical skills, and workplace behaviours, that they need to thrive and succeed in the workplace. In other words, new apprenticeship educators use their skill and expertise to help their apprentices to learn, so they 'know more' and can 'do more'.

REFLECTION POINT

In order to choose the most effective teaching and training methods, resources and approaches, both on- and off-the-job, it is helpful to consider what 'learning' actually is.

- How would you define learning?
- When did you last learn something new?
- How did you know you had learned something?
- How would you know if one of your apprentices had learned something?
- Is learning always observable through a change in behaviour?

What is learning?

Learning is complex and often means different things to different people. Today, many researchers, cognitive scientists and psychologists would agree that learning occurs when there has been a change in our long-term memory, when we have transferred information and experiences from our short-term, or working, memory to the vast storeroom that is our long-term memory. The role of educators, therefore, is to introduce our learners to important new information, knowledge and materials, help them process, make sense and meaning of it, transfer and store it in their long-term memory, and then retrieve it when we need it, for example to perform a skill as part of their job.

Educationalists often talk about learning as the development of a web, or framework, of connected information and related ideas known as 'schema'. When we are able to link new information and material to what we already know, we are able to construct meaning and develop and extend our schemas. This 'learning' helps us to know more, do more and make sense of the world.

FIND OUT MORE

To explore the science behind teaching and how we learn in more detail, there are lots of great resources to support tutors, trainers and coaches.

Teacher, consultant, author and popular edublogger David Didau offers practitioners a range of useful articles, videos and practical ideas on his popular blog 'The Learning Spy' – https://learningspy.co.uk.

The Learning Scientists website (www.learningscientists.org) provides a range of useful free resources to help trainers and tutors understand how to best use their valuable time to help learners, focusing on evidence-based research, rather than working on intuition alone.

Ingle and Duckworth (2013b) consider a number of key learning ideas, or theories of learning, that have influenced the approach of educators over the last 100 years. Let's take a look at three key ideas (Table 3.1):

Table 3.1 Key learning ideas

Learning orientation	What is it?	Possible practical considerations for teachers, tutors and trainers
Behaviourism	A popular view of learning in the early twentieth century, learning is seen as a change in people's behaviour as a result of an action or experience. Learners' behaviour can be determined through the environment and controlled through a 'stimulus-response' approach by the instructor. This 'cause and effect' view of learning is often the result of use of positive and negative reinforcements by tutors, leading to changes in observed learner behaviour. This narrow theory of learning does not acknowledge non-observable learning, changes in thinking or the need for critical thought. Learners respond to their environment rather than being active agents in their own learning.	Although this theory of learning is somewhat outdated, we can still see elements of behaviourism in training rooms today, often focused on behaviour management. For example, the use of praise and rewards to reinforce desirable behaviours demonstrated by apprentices and colleagues. Online learning programmes and apps often award badges and tokens to reinforce 'positive' learning behaviours. Behaviourism focuses on learning as an observable change in new behaviour, often highlighted through shared learning outcomes and targets, for example: 'At the end of the session, apprentices will be able to...' Learning behaviours are developed through practical experience, requiring frequent practice, repetition and reinforcement in the training room and in the workshop, for example.

Social and cognitive constructivism	A much more accepted theory of student-centred learning today, constructivism views learning as something that happens in the mind, a cognitive change in what we remember and comprehend. New knowledge builds on prior learning and what we already know. This new knowledge connects to and builds on our exiting schemas, and helps us to develop new meaning. Learners seek insight by looking at the 'bigger picture' in order to try and make sense of their world. Social constructivism acknowledges the importance of learning by working with others in a social context, for example in the classroom, in the online forum or in the workplace.	Teaching apprentices small chunks of new knowledge will help them to build their schemas so they can use their knowledge at work, for example in developing the skills required to be occupationally competent. Discussions, debates and problem-solving tasks are activities which can be useful to promote critical thinking, reasoning and understanding, to help apprentices learn and make meaning. The use of examples, applied case studies, analogies and metaphors are helpful to build connections between old (prior) knowledge and new knowledge. Opportunities for apprentices to observe, shadow, question and learn from others, for example experienced colleagues, managers and workplace mentors, will be helpful to deepen their understanding and practical skills.
Humanistic/ holistic education	Learning from a humanistic perspective is concerned with developing the 'whole learner' through a more holistic approach to education. Learners are seen as programmed to grow and learn and to want to achieve their full potential. There is a focus on learners' needs, feelings and emotions. A programme of learning should not just focus on cognitive knowledge but also social and emotional development, to make the individual more self-aware, confident, resilient, to become a successful member of society.	Teachers should give time and attention to understanding students' social, emotional and wider learning needs, not just gaps in subject knowledge. If the learner is not confident in their abilities to learn, the teaching of content may not be particularly profitable. Activities which explore learners' own interests and motivations may be useful in shaping effective learning experiences and helping apprentices to see the relevance of their learning to their everyday lives and their workplace. Trainers could use tools and techniques which encourage apprentices to become more self-aware about how they learn, the way they learn, how to be a better learner and how to stay resilient when things go wrong.

Three domains of learning

When thinking about what we want our apprentices to learn, and how best to achieve this, it is helpful to consider three main areas, or domains, of learning, popularised by educational psychologists in the mid to late twentieth century (Bloom et al., 1956; Harrow, 1972; Anderson and Krathwohl, 2000; Figure 3.1).

The **cognitive learning** domain is often associated to the underpinning knowledge, facts and theories that apprentices need to understand, in order to be able to carry out their role. For example, a lead adult care worker may need to develop a secure knowledge and understanding of relevant statutory standards, regulations and codes of practice.

The **affective domain** can be linked to the values, feelings and behaviours that apprentices need to develop in order to carry out their role effectively. For example, a lead adult care worker needs to develop the professional behaviours and values which allow them to provide care and support with kindness, consideration, dignity, empathy and respect.

The **psychomotor domain** can be linked to the practical and technical skills that apprentices need to be able to demonstrate competently and safely in their role, at the required occupational standard. For example, a lead adult care worker needs to develop skills in carrying out fire safety and risk assessment procedures, complete care records clearly and concisely, and demonstrate best practice in hand hygiene.

There is a clear crossover, and overlap, between each of the domains as apprentices will use their developing knowledge and understanding when carrying out and applying their practical skills in the workplace. Their professional behaviours and values will be shaped by their developing understanding of the role and the expectations of their employer and in turn, will be demonstrated through the professional skills they use with their customers, clients and colleagues.

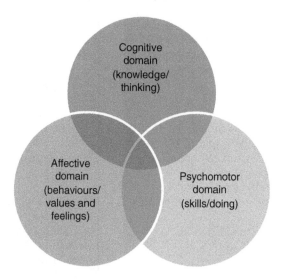

Figure 3.1 Three domains of learning

It is clear to see that new apprenticeships focus on developing all three key learning domains to ensure apprentices are able to demonstrate competence consistently in their role. The following case study explores how Ky's apprenticeship standard combines the essential knowledge, skills and behaviours he needs to develop to be an effective beauty therapist.

CASE STUDY

Ky has been enrolled on his beauty therapist apprenticeship for the last 6 months, working in the spa at a local 4-star country hotel. He attends his training provider's learning centre one day a week for a mix of theory sessions, and practical learning in the training salon.

He sometimes finds the theoretical aspects of his off-the-job training challenging. He much prefers getting hands-on, developing his practical skills in the afternoon sessions in the salon. However, his vocational tutors work hard to make the links between the theory and practice clear. He knows that to be a better therapist, and to impress his employer at the end of his apprenticeship, he needs to develop a confident understanding of the key building blocks of knowledge that therapists need to be able to carry out treatments effectively and safely.

Let's take a look at the links between the knowledge, skills and behaviours in Ky's apprenticeship standard, and how these build on each other (Figure 3.2).

Knowledge (know it):

- the structure and function of the skin and hair
- the hair growth cycle and factors that affect hair growth
- the anatomy and physiology of the body, face, hands, feets, nails and skin
- health and safety legislation and practice
- contraindications and contra-actions
- methods that promote environmental and sustainable working practices
- legal requireemnts, codes of practice, ethics

Skills (show it):

- consult, plan, prepare and perform services and treatments on clients safely, minimising risk of cross contamination, infection or injury
- use products and equipment hyginically and effectively in line with manufacturing guidelines
- correctly use, store and dispose of personal protective equipment
- provide advice and recommendations on the beauty treatments, products, aftercare and appointments.

Behaviours (live it):

- demonstrate a commitment to quality, maintains honesty, integrity and confidentiality
- adapt positively to changing work priorities and patterns when new tasks need to be completed or requirements change
- show clients/customers respect at all times and in all circumstances, demonstrate client empathy, sensitivity and awareness.

Significant and substantial progress over time

Figure 3.2 A summary of knowledge, skills and behaviours (adapted from the level 2 beauty therapist apprenticeship standard, available at: www.instituteforapprenticeships.org/apprenticeship-standards/beauty-therapist)

Ky's vocational tutors explain the importance of developing these building blocks of knowledge to ensure they are secure, so he can apply them to his practical work with clients, developing skill and expertise over time. As he becomes more confident and skilled with different treatments,

(Continued)

(Continued)

procedures and equipment, he becomes more professional, developing high quality, respectful working behaviours to ensure his clients' needs are fully met.

Although he can find much of the theory aspects of his training difficult, Ky is always excited to get back to work after his off-the-job training to practise and apply his new knowledge and skills with clients at the spa. His manager is really supportive and allows him to shadow more experienced therapists to see how they work with clients. When his skills coach visits him at the hotel, he is able to show them how his skills and behaviours have developed. Together, Ky, his coach and manager review his progress and discuss new targets that keep him challenged and moving forward. He's well on track to move through the apprenticeship gateway in the next 9 months.

────── REFLECTION POINT ──────

Consider an apprenticeship standard you are working with and the different elements of the occupational standard that you need to help your apprentices learn.

Identify the different types of knowledge they need to develop, such as the theories of child development or the possible impact of contraindications in beauty therapy. Try to identify the knowledge they need to develop their practical skills, for example how to carry out a back massage, or change a tyre safely and efficiently.

- Now consider what might be the most effective ways to help your apprentices develop the knowledge, understanding, skills and behaviours they need to meet the standard
- Would you use different teaching approaches, methods and activities to develop different types of knowledge and practical skills?
- Would you use different teaching and training approaches with different apprentices?
- Should employers and colleagues use different approaches for on-the-job training to tutor and coaches facilitating off-the-job training?

The role of the new apprentice educator

As we have started to explore, the role of trainers and tutors on apprenticeship programmes is primarily to help and support their apprentices to *learn* substantial new knowledge, understanding and skills. To do this effectively, we must consider the best ways to help apprentices acquire, connect, interpret, construct and make sense of new knowledge and information, store and remember it, and then use it effectively and efficiently to carry out their roles in the workplace. But how should educators approach this process? In their book on teaching and training vocational learners, Ingle and Duckworth (2013a) outline a useful framework for planning how we can best facilitate and support apprentices' learning in training sessions (Figure 3.3).

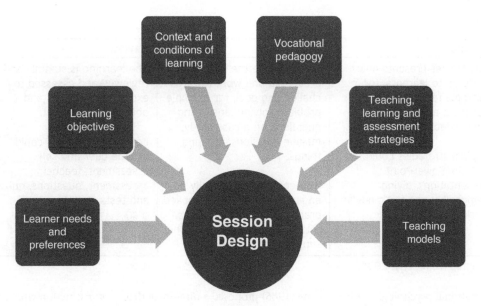

Figure 3.3 A framework for planning effective vocational sessions (Ingle and Duckworth, 2013a)

As we explored in Chapter 2, tutors need to be fully aware of apprentice's starting points and knowledge gaps, and where they need to get to, in order to meet the requirements of the occupational standard. Tutors should also consider the context and conditions for learning, for example:

- off-the-job learning in a whole class groups with other apprentices

- a one-to-one coaching session with the skills coach

- online learning delivered live (synchronously) or self-paced (asynchronously)

- learning on the job by shadowing, observing and imitating experienced colleagues

- learning through reflection during a progress review with the skills coach and employer

- independent learning at home, using a variety of learning resources.

Trainers and tutors should consider carefully the different approaches, tools, strategies, models and pedagogies that will help their apprentices to learn best. Research by the Learning and Skills Network and City and Guilds Centre for Skills Development (Faraday, Overton and Cooper, 2011) identified that many popular models of teaching are neither widely understood nor used in the teaching and training of vocational learners. So, let's take a look at some of the different models and approaches to teaching and training that may be helpful.

Teaching models and approaches

Popular educational author and teacher trainer Geoff Petty (2006) highlights the 'present, apply, review' (PAR) model of teaching as a possible way to structure a session (Table 3.2).

Table 3.2 PAR model

Present	Apply	Review
The trainer presents new material to learners, for example facts, theories, concepts and subject knowledge. Typical strategies could include, PowerPoint presentations, giving demonstrations and modelling worked examples.	Learners use the information presented and work towards a challenging goal, for example problem-solving, answering questions on a case study, making decisions, creating things. Apprentices will typically be engaged in a range of applied, practical, experiential tasks, with different levels of trainer support and guidance.	The learning is summarised, reviewed and assessed to explore if the goals and objectives were met. Learning strategies could include peer and self-assessment, teacher assessment, questions, quizzes and tests.

(Adapted from Petty, 2006)

Educational psychologist Robert Gagne (1985) proposed a nine-stage theory of instruction which may be helpful to trainers in planning and structuring their approach to apprenticeship teaching and training sessions:

(1) Gain learners' attention – make a connection, establish expectations and develop a rapport

(2) Inform learners of the learning objectives – so they know what to expect and why

(3) Recall and retrieve prior learning – to build on their prior knowledge

(4) Present the stimulus – introduce the learning content and new material

(5) Provide learning guidance – by modelling, scaffolding and guiding

(6) Elicit performance – learners should practice and apply to a given task

(7) Provide feedback – on what's working and where correction and improvement is needed

(8) Assess performance – to check learners' understanding and skills and to gain feedback

(9) Enhance retention and transfer – apprentices should be able to use their new learning in new and different contexts, such as the workplace or the end-point assessment

REFLECTION POINT

Think about a group training session you may have taught recently, and a one-to-one training session you may have had with an apprentice.

- Would Gagne's 9-stage model provide a useful model of instruction for both these different types of learning session?
- How long would you spend on each stage?
- What specific teaching methods, tools and resources might you use at each stage?

In 2010, American educator and educational psychologist Professor Barak Rosenshine published an article outlining ten key principles for instruction, based on research in cognitive science and the practice of highly effective teachers. Rosenshine's principles provide a clear and accessible link between research and teaching practice and have proved very popular with new and more experienced teachers and tutors as a useful guide to approaching teaching, learning and assessment in different situations. Table 3.3 outlines the ten key principles and some practical implications for instructors and trainers.

Table 3.3 Practical implications of Rosenshine's (2010) principles in apprenticeships

Principles	Practical implications
1. Daily review	Begin a training session with a short review, around 5-10 minutes, of previous learning. This regular review helps apprentices to retrieve and recall previous learning from their long-term memory, strengthening the connections and deepening their understanding.
2. Present new material and information using small steps	As we only have a very limited amount of working memory space, spend sufficient time presenting new information and material to apprentices in small amounts, or chunks, step by step. You might be using a whiteboard, a visualiser, a shared computer screen or a verbal explanation. Talk out loud as you explain clearly the steps and process you are using to work through examples and models.
3. Ask questions	Questioning apprentices helps them to practice and connect new materials to their prior learning. It also provides you with valuable feedback on what they have understood and where material needs to be covered again. Ask apprentices lots of questions that probe and challenge them to explain their thinking and make connections, not just to confirm they have understood.
4. Provide models	Help apprentices to develop a deeper understanding by providing appropriate prompts, models, worked examples, applied real-life scenarios. Explain examples as you work through them together. Explain any specific steps or stages, processes or procedures. Learners may need significant support at first, through frequent demonstration and explanation.
5. Guide student practice	Spend time guiding apprentices as they practise and rehearse the new material themselves. Support their developing knowledge and skills with prompts, so the new material is not overwhelming, but not too easy. This support can be reduced and withdrawn as apprentices become more confident and move to more independent practice on more complex examples.
6. Check for student understanding	Carry out frequent checks to make sure there are no misconceptions. Observe and question apprentices to

(Continued)

Table 3.3 (Continued)

Principles	Practical implications
	ensure they understand the content, the material, specific processes and procedures. Check for a deeper understanding by asking apprentices to explain how and why. Ask them to provide a rationale or justification, or to summarise the learning. If apprentices are not able to, more time may be needed on direct instruction, modelling or guided practice.
7. Obtain a high success rate	Ensure that all apprentices are mastering the small steps of new material and learning. If too many are not successful, then it may not be time to move on to new content. If apprentices are very successful very quickly, do they know the material already? The content may not be providing sufficient challenge to allow apprentices to develop substantial new knowledge, skills and behaviours. Have you understood their starting points accurately? Can you stretch them further with more challenging content?
8. Provide scaffolds for difficult tasks	Provide apprentices with useful scaffolding and supports that helps them work towards learning challenging new knowledge and skills. This could include models, frameworks, checklists, resources and prompts. These supports should be temporary, and can be removed as apprentices become more confident and independent.
9. Independent practice	In order for apprentices to be successful in the workplace, they need to learn new knowledge, skills and behaviours, but also to use what they have learned with their colleagues, clients and customers. Set apprentices targets, tasks and projects which allows them to practise with increasing independence and confidence, developing and enhancing their level of understanding, speed, precision and skill over time. As they practise again and again, this overlearning helps them to really master the knowledge and practical skills, developing occupational competence and expertise, allowing apprentices to work consistently at a high standard.
10. Weekly and monthly review	Despite effective instruction, apprentices will forget new material, even if they remembered it soon after being taught. Provide opportunities for regular reviews of learning over time, including materials learned last week, last month and last term. This will help learners to rehearse their recall of information, ensuring they know how to find it in their long-term memory, so they can do with without consciously thinking about it. When we have knowledge and skills that we can use fluently and automatically, we free up our working memory to deal with even more new material. The learning continues.

FIND OUT MORE

The American Federation of Teachers published an adapted version of Rosenshein's original article in their journal *American Educator* in 2012. Read the nine-page article and consider how each of the main ten principles can be helpful to guide your approach to teaching the new apprenticeships either in a group, during a one-to-one coaching and review session, online or in the workplace.

www.apprenticeships.today/Rosenshine.

TAKE IT FURTHER

Ex-head teacher, consultant, trainer and popular edublogger, Tom Sherringham (@TeacherHead) has done much to raise the awareness and practical impact of Rosenshine's principles in recent years. His accessible and user-friendly publication 'Rosenshine's Principals in Action' (2019), illustrated by Oliver Cavigliolo, illustrates a range of really useful ways that teachers and trainers can use these principles in their everyday practice.

To find out more, explore the @teacherhead blog: www.teacherhead.com.

CASE STUDY

Mikey is a training consultant for a national training provider. He is new to the role after being made redundant from his previous post, where he worked for almost 20 years as a document production manager for a large firm of solicitors. Mikey is enjoying his new job, using his significant experience and skills to support his caseload of apprentices on the level 3 business administration apprenticeship standard. Mikey visits apprentices in the workplace to carry out progress reviews and to meet with employers. He also delivers training workshops online using video conferencing software. This allows as many apprentices as possible to attend training sessions as they are in different locations across England.

Mikey talks through his presentation slides by sharing his screen with the apprentices. He intro- duces as much content as possible, as they only have online sessions every 3 weeks, and often some apprentices don't log in or have to leave early as they are busy at work. He frequently asks if they have any questions, but they rarely do. When he asks them if they understand the learning material and content, they almost always type 'yes' in the chat box. When Mikey is reviewing their completed assignment and project work, he often finds big gaps in their knowledge. When he visits them in the workplace, he uses the opportunity to go over some of the content from the online sessions. He's disappointed that they often seem unable to recall the material covered, even though they had no questions at the time.

Mikey is worried that they are not developing the knowledge and skills they need to be able to pass their end-point assessments. He is mindful not to challenge them too much though, as they are always really busy at work and often struggle to get time away from their desks to meet with him. Meetings are often brief and most of the time is spent completing review records which he must get completed for audit purposes. It's always difficult to get to speak with the apprentice's manager too when he visits. Mikey's own supervisor has told him not to make a fuss as the most important thing is to make sure the apprentices stay on the programme.

REFLECTIVE QUESTIONS

- Thinking about the models and principles of instruction we have explored above, what changes would you advise Mikey to make to his approach to training?
- What support should Mikey seek to ensure that his apprentices have clear expectations about what is expected on a new apprenticeship programme?
- What conversation would you have with the apprentices' manager to ensure they are likely to be successful on the apprenticeship?

Taking an evidence-based approach

Rosenshine's principles provide an accessible bridge between educational research, and the practical actions that teachers and tutors can take in their everyday practice. One thing that almost every tutor and trainer is short of is time, and therefore effort invested in facilitating effective, high-quality training for apprentices needs to have the most profitable impact on their learning and their progress over time. By taking an evidence-based, research-informed approach, tutors, trainers and coaches can cut through the latest fads, gimmicks and pseudoscience that often leads to 'initiative fatigue', and instead choose the methods, tools and approaches that really do help apprentices to know more and do more.

For example, many apprenticeship assessors have previously spent much time exploring apprentices' 'learning styles' and how their training methods should be adapted to meet their learners' preferred styles. Although very popular, research tells us that the idea that learners learn best through materials and information presented through a mainly visual, auditory, or kinaesthetic style (VAK) or mode is not based in science, is unlikely to improve learning and is highly likely to be a waste of tutors' valuable time. Time would be much better spent understanding the key knowledge that apprentices need to learn and planning an approach to learning that helps them to remember.

FIND OUT MORE

Take some time to explore how learning styles became such a popular idea for many tutors and trainers, and the science that helps us to understand why there are better ways to focus our time and efforts in helping apprentices to learn better.

Do Visual, Auditory, and Kinesthetic Learners Need Visual, Auditory, and Kinesthetic Instruction? by Professor of Cognitive Psychology Daniel T. Willingham: www.aft.org/ae/summer2005/willingham.

Learning Styles: Time to Move On by Emeritus Professor of Education Frank Coffield: www.apprenticeships.today/move-on.

Focus on learning

Professor Rob Coe (2013) reminds educators that learning happens when people have to 'think hard'. Do your apprentices have to think hard in your training sessions? We might cover lots of content and show many presentation slides, apprentices might take the time to make lots of notes, but does this automatically lead to great learning? Unless information and knowledge has made it to the long-term memory, as we have explored, these activities may look like engaging teaching but not necessarily lead to good learning. Professor Coe identifies six possible indicators to look out for in our training session that we might mistake for good learning:

(1) Students are busy: lots of work is done (especially written work)

(2) Students are engaged, interested, motivated

(3) Students are getting attention: feedback, explanations

(4) Classroom is ordered, calm, under control

(5) Curriculum has been 'covered' (i.e. presented to students in some form)

(6) (At least some) students have supplied correct answers (whether or not they really understood them or could reproduce them independently).

So, rather than thinking too much about teaching, where most apprentices may be engaged and 'busy', we should instead focus on effective *learning*. Which strategies and methods should you use in your training, coaching and review sessions to help your apprentices learn best? Keeping up to date with educational research and learning theories will help you to prioritise your precious time to focus on the tools, strategies and resources which are low in effort, but have the highest impact on apprentices' learning and their rate of progress.

REFLECTION POINT

Think about a recent group training session you may have been involved with recently.

- How much effort did you put in compared to how much effort the apprentices put in?
- Did apprentices have to think hard?

(Continued)

> *(Continued)*
> - Were apprentices *learning* or were they just busy? How do you know?
> - What might you do differently next time to ensure all your time and effort has impact, leading to great learning?

The Great Teaching Toolkit (2020), from Evidence Based Education, has reviewed existing research studies to identify four key priorities or dimensions, and associated practical advice, to guide practitioners who want to help their student learn more. Let's explore each of the four priorities and what this may mean practically for you in your role (Table 3.4).

Table 3.4 Four dimensions of great teaching

Dimensions of great teaching	Practical implications of trainers and tutors
1. Understand the content you are teaching and how it is learnt	• Apprenticeship trainers need to ensure they have a deep and secure knowledge and understanding of what they are teaching. Keeping up to date with the latest developments in the occupational sector is important. • Trainers should be aware of the common misconceptions and challenges that apprentices often have with specific aspects of the curriculum, and how to overcome these. • Trainers should know how the curriculum links together and builds sequentially to develop knowledge and skills over time.
2. Create a supportive environment for learning	• Trainers need to work hard to build positive relationships with their apprentices, developing a culture of trust so they feel confident to take risks in their learning, have a go, make mistakes and ask for help when they need it. • Trainers should have high expectations for their apprentices, challenging them appropriately to go further and deeper in their learning. • Trainers should create a positive climate of learning, sensitive to apprentices' individual needs and pressures (at work or at home), motivating them to keep going and celebrating success.
3. Manage the classroom to maximise the opportunity to learn	• Trainers should make best use of the valuable time they have with apprentices to maximise learning. Consider setting pre-learning

Dimensions of great teaching	Practical implications of trainers and tutors
	activities for apprentices to watch, read or review before the session, so you can use your expertise to question, challenge, correct and guide - not just present information. • Give apprentices clear instructions, reinforce and recognise positive learning behaviours, attitudes and behaviours, and use routines to establish expectations.
4. Present content, activities and interactions that activate students' hard thinking	• Trainers should understand apprentices' prior knowledge and starting points, in order to match tasks to their needs and readiness. • Trainers should explain new ideas clearly and concisely, building and connecting ideas to what apprentices have learnt previously. • Use applied examples, demonstrations and modelling to support and scaffold new learning, gradually removing the support as learners become more secure and independent. • Use tasks which allow learners to practise, rehearse, embed and apply their knowledge and skills, so they can master them with fluency and consistency. • Use questioning, review, revision and checking techniques frequently to get all apprentices thinking hard and to prevent forgetting over time.

(Adapted from 'The Great Teaching Toolkit', 2020)

FIND OUT MORE

Explore the toolkit at: www.greatteaching.com and consider the practical advice on how to plan and deliver training sessions that have the biggest impact on learning and progress over time.

Finding out what works

The Education Endowment Fund (EEF) is charity funded by the Department for Education, and the UK government's 'What Works' Centre for Education. The EEF fund research projects and carry out research evidence reviews to find out what is likely to work the best in education. They produce a comprehensive teaching and learning toolkit which provides a summary of international evidence on teaching school-age learners, but also a dedicated post-16 research strand. The evidence reviews explore the costs of different approaches and the impact they could have on learners' progress.

Four of the most effective approaches relevant to apprenticeship are as follows (Table 3.5).

Educational research does not provide a set checklist, or fixed recipe, of the specific steps that we must all follow in order for our teaching and training to lead to great learning. The different contexts of apprenticeship training, of individual apprentices and their vocational tutors, and the workplaces that apprentices operate in, are so diverse and complex that what might work for one apprentice may not lead to great learning for another in a different context.

Table 3.5 Four effective learning approaches

1. Providing feedback	Evidence suggests that the impact of providing learners with clear, specific and accurate feedback is one of the most effective things that trainers and tutors can do. Whilst this sounds straight forward, the quality of feedback can vary significantly. We will explore how to give effective feedback in the next chapter in more detail.
2. Metacognition and self-regulation	Are your apprentices passive passengers in their learning, or are they active participants in their own learning journey? How well do your apprentices understand how they learn best? Are they able to independently plan, monitor and evaluate their own learning and make changes to their plans when they need to? Metacognition and self-regulation activities focus on helping apprentices to learning about how they learn best and how they can be more effective independent lifelong learners. We will explore the importance of metacognition and self-regulation more in Chapter 5.
3. Home learning	How often do you set your apprentices learning activities to be completed before or after a training session? Encouraging learners to complete meaningful research tasks, projects and practice activities outside of training sessions and workplace visits may help them to learn more, and make more significant and substantial progress.
4. Cooperative learning	More than just 'group work', cooperative learning requires each member of a learning group to collaborative effectively towards a clear shared goal. Apprentices are interdependent on each other, so they 'sink or swim' together in their achievement of the activity or task which has been set. In a cooperative learning approach, everyone must pull their weight and play their part; there is no hiding place like we sometimes see in less structured group work. Apprentices might find it helpful to be allocated a specific role, for example team leader, researcher, producer, facilitator, so they have accountability in the learning and its outcome.

The research does, however, present us with a range of approaches and tools that are more likely to be effective with our learners. The research can guide our options and choices so that we focus our efforts and energies on tools and strategies that are more likely to be the most profitable in helping our learners to know more and do more.

REFLECTION POINT

Think about each of the four priorities suggested by Evidence Based Education in The Great Teaching Toolkit (2020), and the four learning approaches highlighted by the EEF above. Carry out a self-assessment exploring to what extent you already use and integrate these methods in your professional practice, where appropriate and where you might have opportunities to experiment and trial them further.

Training approach self-assessment 1 = not at all like me … 5 = very much like me	Score 1-5
• I understand my apprentices' prior knowledge and starting points, in order to provide new materials and activities which match needs and readiness.	☐
• I explain new ideas clearly and concisely, building and connecting ideas to what my apprentices have learnt previously.	☐
• I use applied examples, demonstrations, modelling and support to scaffold new learning, gradually removing the support as apprentices become more secure and independent.	☐
• I use evidence-based teaching strategies to avoid the pitfalls of techniques and resources which may engage learners and keep them busy, but which don't lead to thinking hard and good learning.	☐
• I am aware of the common misconceptions and challenges that my apprentices have with specific aspects of the curriculum I teach, and I have a plan to help them overcome these.	☐
• I set my apprentices learning tasks to complete before and after training sessions and there is a high expectation that these must be completed.	☐
• I spend time developing a culture of trust so my apprentices feel confident to take risks in their learning, have a go, make mistakes and ask for help when they need it.	☐
• I embed opportunities for apprentices to work together on cooperative and collaborative learning tasks, giving individuals specific roles so they are fully accountable.	☐
• I encourage my apprentices to develop their metacognitive and learning-to-learn skills, so they can become more reflective, strategic and independent learners.	☐

Developing apprentices' applied English and maths skills

As we explored in Chapter 2, a key part of a new apprenticeship is to further develop apprentices' applied English and mathematics skills, and often their ICT skills too where relevant. This is important to ensure they are able to carry out their roles and responsibilities at work confidently, efficiently and safely. Apprentices may also need to develop their skills in order to help them achieve formal qualifications, for example Functional Skills assessments at level 1 or 2, as a requirement of going through the gateway, and being able to attempt their end-point assessments.

Whether or not apprentices already hold suitable formal qualifications, the focus of their learning programme should be to help them close any skills gaps that have been identified through the initial and diagnostic assessments. As we saw with Niamh in the earlier case study, even where learners have formal qualifications, they may well still struggle with their use of English and maths in a range of applied situations, for example (Table 3.6).

Apprentices may attend specific teaching sessions with qualified English and mathematics tutors, in order to develop their understanding of key concepts and processes, and to practise their skills. Tutors could demonstrate worked examples on the board, provide a range of part-completed activities to guide learners' practise and then offer a range of mock and practice assessments to develop learners' confidence and independence.

An increasingly common approach taken by many learning providers is to subscribe to online learning activities, resources and materials, which can support and guide learners in the development of skills, mapped to their specific needs identified through initial and diagnostic assessment. Whilst this

Table 3.6 Applying English and mathematics skills in the workplace

Applied English skills	Applied maths skills
- being able to write a formal letter to customers which is well presented and uses suitable language.	- being able to calculate how much sales have increased or the discount a customer can have on a purchase, as a percentage.
- being able to compose an accurate email to clients that communicates key ideas and options clearly, with correct use of spelling, grammar and punctuation.	- being able to calculate the area of a room to work out the amount of floor covering needed for a job quote.
- being able to read a range of detailed and complex reports and documents to compare information, ideas and opinions with confidence.	- being able to add, subtract, multiply and divide decimals up to two decimal places, when calculating a quote for a new client.
- being able to take part in a discussion at work, asking relevant questions and expressing an opinion.	- being able to represent data and statistics in a table, chart and graph for a management presentation.

approach may be effective for some apprentices, for example allowing them to work at their own pace, in their own time, other learners may need more structured training, advice and guidance to help get them started, particularly if they lack confidence. Skills coaches should take the time to understand how apprentices feel about using online resources independently, check they are able to log in and access the right type of activities that will address their skills gaps the best and regularly assess their progress in reviews and face-to-face training sessions to check if they have really learnt the skills they need and are able to use them in different contexts.

Vocational tutors can also develop their apprentice's applied skills by embedding suitable English and maths material and activities, where relevant, into occupational teaching sessions. This will help apprentices to see the importance of developing their skills as part of their role at work. For example:

- a customer service apprentice needs to develop their writing skills in order to be able to communicate with customers via email and on social media professionally and accurately. A mistake could be embarrassing and impact on the company reputation

- an apprentice material cutter will need to develop their mathematical skills in order to estimate and calculate the materials required to complete the job. An incorrect estimate could be a costly mistake.

Tutors should harness all relevant opportunities to reinforce and develop apprentices' applied English and mathematics skills, but avoid trying to 'shoe-horn' them into training sessions where they lack purpose. This will use up valuable training time that could be better spent on helping apprentices get to grips with vocational material.

FIND OUT MORE

The Education and Training Foundation (ETF) offers a range of free resources and courses to help apprenticeship tutors and coaches embed English and maths effectively in their delivery. For more information, visit: www.apprenticeships.today/English-Maths.

Working together

For a new apprenticeship to have the biggest impact on learning, training providers and employers must work together to plan and deliver a challenging programme of training and development that builds on apprentices' starting points and enables them to make significant and substantial progress in developing new knowledge, skills and behaviours.

As we explored in Chapter 2, the link between on- and off-the-job training is a crucial one. Training providers, apprentices and their employers should all work closely together to deliver a high-quality programme of training and work experience that complement each other. Employers should ensure that apprentices have a range of opportunities to apply the new knowledge and understanding they have developed through vocational training sessions, online learning and one-to-one coaching. Let's explore a few ways that training providers and employers can work together to deliver an effective apprenticeship training programme:

- managers can allocate their apprentices specific work projects that allow them to build on, apply and consolidate the knowledge and skills they have learned in the classroom

- workplace mentors or buddies can monitor and support apprentices as they demonstrate and practise the technical skills they are learning, with greater speed and accuracy

- training providers can build on and extend training carried out in the workplace by setting assignments or presentations which help apprentices to reflect on the purpose and value of the training

- skills coaches can ask employers about naturally occurring opportunities where apprentices will need to apply their English and maths skills in the workplace, so they can devise relevant activities and guidance.

The planned programme may need to be adapted during delivery, to ensure it continues to meet the needs of apprentices. For example, apprentices may make faster or slower than expected progress in their learning, and may need more support or additional challenge to ensure they continue to learn effectively. The apprentice may need to undertake a wider range of duties or responsibilities than anticipated, in order to ensure they are able to develop the breadth and depth of skills required by the occupational standard.

CASE STUDY

Reena works for a two-form entry primary school and is completing her level 3 teaching assistant apprenticeship. Reena loves working with reception and Year 1 children the most but Tara, her skills coach, is concerned that she is not getting a broad enough experience working with children across the school, in order to develop her knowledge, skills and behaviours fully. At one of her regular review visits, Tara discusses possible adaptations to the training plan with Reena's line manager Paul. Together they identify how Reena can gain more experience working with older children in Key Stage 2 (KS2), which will develop her experience particularly in the areas of behaviour management, special education needs and social and emotional support. Reena will shadow a KS2 higher-level teaching assistant and co-lead an intervention group with a small number of children. Reena is pleased with the new challenge and the opportunity to try out different roles. The experience will also give her a change to capture some additional evidence for her end-point assessment portfolio and discussion, so she can showcase her breadth of skills.

The importance of high expectations

For over 50 years, psychologists and researchers have been exploring the importance of having high expectations of learners and what they can achieve in their education. Research identifies that when educators work effectively together, and have high levels of confidence in their abilities to help their learners make significant progress, this often becomes the reality and positive impact is found. Trainers, tutors and coaches should also have high expectations about what their apprentices can achieve, with the right training, level of challenge, support and guidance. Studies have shown (Rosenthal and Jacobsen, 1968) than when teachers believe their learners are likely to make substantial progress in their learning, they were more willing to challenge them further with additional content and learning material, more willing to question them and encourage a contribution, and more willing to provide learners with specific, corrective feedback when they got things wrong. As a result, the teacher's high expectations became a self-fulfilling prophecy (the so-called Pygmalion Effect), as learners profited from the additional input and feedback from their teachers.

Conversely, where teachers and trainers have low expectations of what their learners are capable of, it often leads to less favourable outcomes and limited progress (the 'Golem Effect'). Tutors who feel that their learners will not be able to cope with or profit from more content, additional challenge and detailed feedback tend not to provide these, resulting in less challenge and slower progress. Whilst the message seems clear and obvious, it can be difficult to maintain high expectations for our apprentices when they may struggle with new concepts, get things wrong at first and find it difficult to get time off work to really focus on their learning. Apprentices may also lack confidence, and have low expectations, of their own abilities to learn, develop and grow, even when they are more than capable of being challenged further with the right support.

Training providers may be cautious not to challenge apprentices too much in case they decide not to continue with their apprenticeship, leading to implications for funding and qualification achievement rate data. If apprentices have not been recruited with sufficient guidance, clarity and integrity, they may feel that their apprenticeship is a quick and easy route to accreditation of existing skills and competencies, rather than a rigorous and challenging programme of training and work experience to develop significant and substantial new learning.

TAKE IT FURTHER

If you are interested to know more about the research behind teacher's high expectations of their students, explore one of the key research studies *'Pygmalion In The Classroom'* by Professor of Psychology Robert Rosenthal, and Dr. Lenore Jacobsen. Find out more by watching this short YouTube video: www.apprenticeships.today/Pygmalion.

Professor John Hattie has carried out significant work to explore what research suggests has the biggest influences on student achievement. His research, Visible Learning, has examined over 1,600 meta-analyses, comprising more than 95,000 studies, involving 300 million students around the world. The impact of collective teacher efficacy, defined as 'the shared belief by a group of teachers in a particular educational environment that they have the skills to positively impact student outcomes', is identified as one of the biggest influences on student achievement. Find out more: www.visiblelearningmetax.com.

The Goldilocks effect: getting the level of learning just right

High expectations really matter if we want our apprentice to make significant progress from their starting points. We must also be careful not to confuse high expectations with unrealistic learning goals and aspirations, however. Challenging our learners too much too soon, without the right amount of support, could overload apprentices, undermine their confidence and increase feelings of anxiety and failure. If the learning is too easy, apprentices may feel that we have low expectations of what they are capable of, leading to low expectations of themselves. Without sufficient challenge, they may get bored or become distracted, perhaps leading to poor attendance or behaviour, and slow progress.

Just as Goldilocks wants to find the bowl of porridge that wasn't too hot or too cold, we want our apprentices to engage with learning which has a level of support and challenge which is 'just right' to build on their current level of knowledge and skills. Professor Mihaly Csikszentmihalyi's (2002) studies into 'flow' and optimal challenge identify the need for teachers and trainers to find the right balance between how much we challenge our learners based on their existing skills. When apprentices are engaged in learning in this optimal zone, content and material is not so easy that they are learning very little which is new (too cold), but is not so difficult or complex that they become overly confused, lost or overloaded (too hot) (Figure 3.4).

— REFLECTION POINT —

Think about a one of your apprentices that you are currently training and supporting.

- How do you ensure that the level of learning is pitched just right?
- How would you know if the learning is too easy or too challenging?
- What could you do to regulate the level of learning back into the optimal zone?
- What could your apprentices do to get themselves back in this optimal zone of learning and performance?

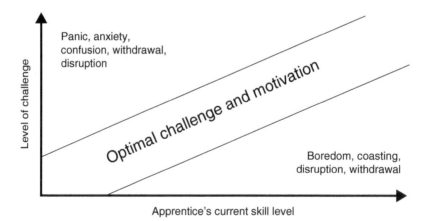

Figure 3.4 Optimal challenge (adapted from Csikszentmihalyi, 2002)

When we are able to pitch learning at the right level for apprentices, we often find learners' motivation for learning, and performance, is at its best. However, if we don't get this balance right, we may find that learning is too complex, causing 'cognitive overload'. This can happen when:

- the quantity of material introduced is too much, overloading the working memory

- the new learning material is provided all at once, without breaking it down into manageable chunks

- the provided material is too complex and difficult for learners' current level of skill and understanding

- learners do not have the support, guidance and scaffolding they need to work through the new content step by step

- learning materials include unnecessarily confusing and distracting information which affects learners' attention and focus.

Beware the 'curse of knowledge'

Apprentices undoubtedly benefit from the advice, guidance and explicit instruction from their vocational experts, many of whom have spent years developing and perfecting their occupational skills, competence and expertise. As the expert, however, it may be difficult to get the level of learning 'just right' for novice apprentices with little prior knowledge and experience. As Professor Paul Kirschner and Dr Carl Hendrick (2020) discuss in their book *How Learning Happens*, a beginner is not a little expert; they know less and think differently to experts. Tutors and trainers need to consider which teaching and learning approaches will work best for their apprentices who have little prior knowledge and experience of their occupational role and vocational subject. They should proactively differentiate their instructional methods, being conscious that as experts, they may well have forgotten the small steps and basic instructions that many beginners need to acquire knowledge when they 'just aren't getting it'.

Tutor and trainers should use frequent ongoing assessment and reflection to ensure that apprentices are not overloaded, or coasting, in their learning. If apprentices are never making mistakes and always get top marks in assessments, this could be an indicator that they are not being sufficiently challenged. They may quickly become bored and may see little point in completing the learning set or attending training they feel has little value. If, however, they are not grasping key concepts, making few contributions in sessions, not answering questions and are making very slow progress, this could be an indication they are in the 'panic zone'. Action will be needed by trainers, or apprentices, to regulate learning back into the optimal zone.

As we see in Figure 3.5, the aim is to keep learning in this 'sweet spot', the golden learning zone, when apprentices have to think hard and work hard, as it is this cognitive strain that will help them to develop their schema, so they know more and can do more.

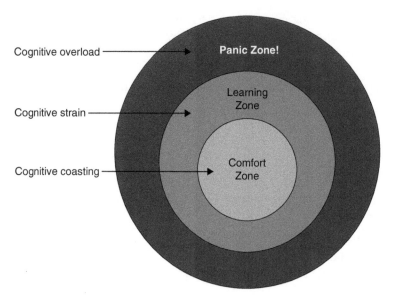

Figure 3.5 Comfort zone model (adapted from Pannicucci, 2007)

— TAKE IT FURTHER —

Psychologist Professor John Sweller has been researching Cognitive Load Theory (CLT) since the 1980s. This is an important theory for instructors, trainers and coaches, as it helps to explain why our learners may become overloaded by tasks and materials which may be too complex for their working memories to handle. As a result, they may become confused, frustrated, upset, embarrassed or even disruptive.

When driving your car, do you ever turn the radio off, or tell your passengers to stop talking for a moment while you reserve park into a tight space? Sometimes we need to reduce the amount of information and distractions our mind has to deal with in order to concentrate and complete a given task. CLT identifies that every mental task we complete produces a given load. This load can become too much to deal with if the task is too demanding, or we don't have the resources we need to support us. These resources could be internal, for example our existing prior knowledge and skills, or external, for example the practical resources that could be used for support, such as a calculator when carrying out complex calculation, or parking sensors and mirrors to help us to judge that reserve parking manoeuvre!

CLT also has implications for how we present our learning materials, to try and reduce the demand on our learners' working memory, by cutting out any unnecessary information or images which may be distracting or split our attention. Linked to CLT, dual coding theory suggests we have two main channels to try and help our working memories process the information we need - the verbal channel and the visual channel. If we present key information in pictorial or graphical form, along with a verbal explanation, this may help our learners select, organise and interpret the information more effectively.

WHAT DOES THIS MEAN FOR TRAINERS?

- Break information down into manageable chunks appropriate to learners' prior knowledge and starting points
- Highlight external learning resources which apprentices can use to support their learning, for example a glossary of new technical language, partially completed examples, calculators, dictionaries, checklists for completing tasks
- Avoid having too much text on presentation slides and then talking over the slides as learners are trying to read them! This is often difficult for the working memory to process at once
- Try using carefully selected graphics and pictures alongside key text and key words to use both the verbal and visual channels, for example diagrams, flow charts, infographics, timelines, cartoons.

Find out more

Professor Dylan Wiliam has described cognitive load theory as 'the single most important thing for teachers to know'. To explore CLT in more detail, and the practical implications for practice, explore Oliver Lovell's (2020) book *Cognitive Load Theory in Action*.

CASE STUDY

Alia is undertaking an assistant accountant apprenticeship, where she will also gain her AAT Level 3 Advance Diploma. Her training provider offered her different study options, such as live online classes, student-led on demand eLearning modules or a face-to-face class with a tutor. Alia finds she lacks the motivation to study online, so opted to undertake her training via a classroom session one day per week. She also has access to a range of study texts and online activities that she can use to support her learning between sessions.

In the class, Alia finds some of the content very straightforward, such as using IT systems and packages to enter accounting transactions and produce reports. She has been using these packages at work for some time now and has a great line manager who has given her lots of support and time to practise. She finds the pace of learning in these sessions slow, as other learners in the class have not used accounting packages very much and the trainer takes lots of time to go through the software functions in great detail.

Alia really starts to struggle when it comes to learning about indirect tax, for example completing VAT returns and applying relevant regulatory and legislation requirements. She finds the tutor moves through complex content very quickly, and doesn't give her enough time to work through the different exercises in class. She finds the concepts really difficult to apply accurately, getting some tasks right but many others wrong. She feels she is getting behind and feels embarrassed when she doesn't know the answer straightaway and everyone else in the class seems to.

(Continued)

(Continued)

REFLECTIVE QUESTIONS

Alia is clearly not always operating in the 'learning zone' for different parts of her apprenticeship and professional qualification.

- What could her **tutor** do to regulate Alia's learning, so she is not coasting or panicking?
- What could **Alia** do to regulate her own learning back into the learning zone, so she is challenged but not overloaded and getting left behind?

Instructor differentiation or apprentice self-regulation?

One way to try and ensure our apprentices are suitably challenged is to differentiate learning. This is to provide learning content and material, tasks, activities and questions which are more accessible or more complex, depending on apprentices' starting points and current levels of competency. This can be very challenging in a group training situation, when many apprentices may well have quite different levels of prior knowledge and understanding.

Trying to differentiate learning for every single apprentice in every session is likely to be unrealistic; however, we may also pitch to the level wrong, under- or overestimate the level of challenge apprentices need and could encourage some apprentices to become dependent on their tutors and instructors. As we will explore further in Chapter 5, developing learners' metacognitive skills will help them to become more self-aware, and to learn about how they learn best themselves. When instructors create the right conditions for learning, apprentices will be able to self-regulate more effectively, using the additional resources and support available when required, or seeking out additional challenging projects, research and reading when necessary. This will help them to ensure the level of learning is just right for them, at that time, in that particular area of learning. In this way, we help apprentices to develop the independent learning and thinking skills they will need to flourish in the workplace, when they need to use their initiative, think on their feet, respond to unforeseen challenges and deal with problems.

Activating apprentices

As we explored earlier with different theories of learning, encouraging apprentices to make connections between their prior knowledge and new material will help them learn and remember, so they can develop their occupational competency and use and apply new skills when needed. In their useful book on generative learning (2020), Zoe Enser and Mark Enser draw on the work of Fiorella and Mayer (2015), to highlight eight useful practical activities that learners can be encouraged to engage in, to help them create meaningful learning and develop the transferable skills required by employers.

Table 3.7 explores some of these useful learning strategies and their possible application with apprentices.

Table 3.7 Learning strategies and applications

Generative learning strategies	What might apprentices do?	Applied example
Summarising	Encourage apprentices to generate a brief written or verbal summary of the main ideas covered in a training session, perhaps asking them to identify key points and make links between theory and practice. To make this more challenging, add additional parameters, such as a word count or time limit, to really focus learners on choosing the most important ideas and links in their summary.	For example, at the end of a theory session, hairdressing apprentices could be asked to summarise in their own words, the links between natural growth patterns of the hair, cutting angles and resulting weight distribution.
Mapping	Apprentices could be asked to generate a mind map or concept map, to organise their thoughts and to make links and connections. Concept maps can help to illustrate how a given concept links to other concepts, people, events, information and ideas. Mapping can help learners to visualise connections and to critically reflect on these, their importance and relevance.	For example, an operational firefighter could complete a mind map to reinforce the links and relationships between community safety and prevention awareness.
Drawing	Apprentices could be asked to generate a drawing representation of the key learning points from a training session, or to create a diagram from a written procedure, process or policy. This would help them to select the key learning points, and integrate and organise the concepts with their prior knowledge.	For example, an apprentice marketing manager could be asked to create a diagram exploring the extended marketing mix and how it could be applied to a specific case study product or service.
Self-explaining	Apprentices could be asked to explain their learning choices, judgements and actions in the classroom or the	For example, a digital support technician apprentice could be encouraged to explain verbally their

(Continued)

Table 3.7 (Continued)

Generative learning strategies	What might apprentices do?	Applied example
	workplace. Instructors or mentors could use a range of reflective questions to encourage learners to explain what they have learnt, why they have approached a task in a particular way, what the advantages and disadvantages of a particular method might be.	approach to diagnosing digital problems, and how they provided end-user support, and what the outcome was.
Teaching	The best way to learn something is to teach it to someone else! Whilst this may not always be true, there is a body of research to suggest encouraging our learners to teach something they are studying to someone else can be a useful learning approach. Workplace mentors could ask their apprentices to 'teach' them something about their role and the project they are working on, or trainers could nominate an apprentice to read a particular chapter, or watch a relevant video clip, on a suitable topic or concept, and then teach this to the rest of the group.	For example, an apprentice florist could be asked to watch a YouTube clip about common indicators of pests and disease and then teach their peers about the possible action that should be taken if they are discovered.
Enacting	Apprentices may learn certain concepts, processes and practical skills through imitation, moving, doing and acting out. This is clearly very helpful for mastering the skills required for practical occupations, but enacting could also be used by less practical areas where apprentices can reinforce more theoretical and cognitive ideas through enacting.	For example, a hospitality team member apprentice can learn about the service touch-points by enacting the customer journey through a restaurant.

── TAKE IT FURTHER ──

A useful framework to encourage learners to summarise their learning is to introduce them to Cornell notes, a note-taking system popularised by Professor Walter Pauk at Cornell University.

Cues / Questions / Key ideas	Notes

Summary – what I learnt today

This is a note-taking protocol where learners structure their note-taking page into key words or concepts, more detailed notes, and a summary box at the bottom of the page. When reviewing, learners can use the summary box. When self-testing, learners can use just the key words column as a prompt or cue to practice retrieving the information from their long-term memory.

To find out more about the system, visit the dedicated information pages from Cornell University: www.apprenticeships.today/Cornell.

Teaching with technology

One way to encourage apprentices to actively engage with learning, construct knowledge and generate meaning and understanding is through the use of technology enhanced learning, or 'EdTech'. Many apprenticeship programmes make extensive use of online technologies in a wide variety of different ways:

- **Interactive online learning** *(synchronous)* **training sessions** – training could be delivered in specific virtual classrooms, or via online video conferencing platforms such as Microsoft Teams, Zoom, Google Meet, Skype, WebEx and many more. Apprentices log in at a set time and undertake their vocational learning with a trainer and other learners in real time, from the comfort of their home or workplace. This would be considered off-the-job learning as it is time away from an apprentice's work role to develop their knowledge and skills. Often, assessors and skills coaches may also use online video conferencing software to carry out progress reviews with their apprentice's and their managers. Table 3.8 explores some of the advantages and disadvantages in carrying out off-the-job training in online synchronous trainer-led sessions.

- **Self-directed** *(asynchronous)* **distance learning materials** – sometimes also described a self-directed distance learning, these materials may be hosted on a virtual learning environment (VLE), such as Moodle, Canvas, Blackboard, SmartVLE, PebblePad and many more. They are available anytime, anyplace, for apprentices to log in and work through activities at their own pace. As we explored earlier, many providers often provide materials and resources to support the development of learners' English and maths skills through e-learning systems. Self-paced e-learning materials may not motivate all apprentices, however, and many may be slow to complete the activities set without the expectation of the 'trainer in the room'. An apprenticeship cannot be delivered by self-directed learning in its entirety.

- **Work-based systems** – many employers make use of corporate training systems, and intranets, to provide their employees with mandatory training that they must complete, for example health and safety, manual handling, safeguarding, data protection and equality and diversity.

- **Informal technologies** – many apprentices may also make use of freely available technologies to support their learning through research and communication, for example:

   - using a YouTube video on how to complete a practical task

   - being part of a WhatsApp messenger group to chat with instructors or other learners

   - participating in a social media group with other learners on Facebook

   - searching on Google Scholar to explore theories and frameworks.

Table 3.8 Advantages and disadvantages of online synchronous training sessions

Advantages	Disadvantages
• Engage apprentices in real time and easily monitor attendance and engagement.	• Not all apprentices may have access to a reliable device at the time of the session.
• With cameras on, monitor body language and non-verbal communication cues to adapt the session as required.	• Internet connections may not be reliable enough or sufficient to participate fully in the session, e.g. streaming video clips.
• Immediately respond to individual questions, test understanding and clarify misconceptions as the arise.	• A live online class can be as (if not more) disruptive as a face-to-face class and requires clear guidelines and protocols.
• Carry out online assessments to get instant feedback to adjust delivery or content as required.	• Apprentices may be reluctant to use their cameras and microphones, leading to very one-way, didactic tutor delivery.

Blended, hybrid and 'flipped' learning

For some apprenticeship programmes, the off-the-job training might take place online with a mix of interactive and self-directed distance learning, and online reviews and visits from assessors and coaches. For others, learning may take place face-to-face in a classroom at a local college or training provider for example, with workplace visits from the training consultant. For most apprentices, however, a more blended approach will often be taken, with a mix of online and face-to-face teaching, assessment and support. Figure 3.6 explores how TEL can contribute to the quality of training in any and all of these delivery modes.

A hybrid approach to learning can happen when the trainer has some learners face-to-face in the classroom and others joining live online through video conferencing software. The trainer will need to ensure that the camera and audio are set up to capture the necessary material and delivery, but also to use technologies which link the different learners together. For example, learners in the classroom could use their own digital devices to join in with live polls or use of online collaborative documents, so the group can work together regardless of mode of study.

The so-called 'flipped learning' or 'flipped classroom' approach is where teachers create the conditions where learners can engage in good-quality learning materials before the live classroom session. This is a pedagogical approach rather than a strictly technological one, however, as learners could engage in print-based materials, such as reading an article, case study or text-book chapter to gain some new knowledge, or it could be using technology, such as watching a video on the VLE or YouTube or completing some interactive e-learning modules.

By engaging in knowledge content, and sometimes online quizzes and tests, *before* the live classroom session, this frees up time and space for the trainer to use instructional approaches and activities that will help learners to transfer this knowledge to their long-term memory, for example modelling, questioning, discussing, correcting and summarising. In this sense, the main purpose of the session has been 'flipped' from a traditional one of content delivery to one of feedback, clarification and challenge.

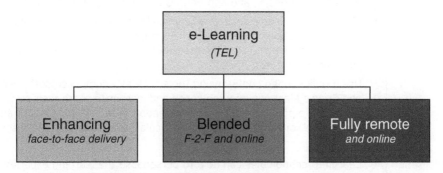

Figure 3.6 Technology-enhanced learning (adapted from Garrison and Kanuka, 2004)

Learning first – technology second

Well-selected technologies can be used to enhance the standard of instruction, the level of meaningful apprentice engagement and the quality of their learning, in all these different modes and models of delivery. Technology can also distract learners, and whilst it may help to make the session fun and engaging, this does not necessarily always translate into good learning. The use of learning technologies can also take valuable time, and depending on your level of skill, it may be a better use of your precious time if it were spent on providing apprentices with specific feedback or planning appropriately challenging training sessions. Therefore, the focus should always be on the *learning* first, and the *technology* second.

REFLECTION POINT

Reflecting on the different models of learning and principles of instruction we have explored in this chapter:

- how could your time be spent most profitably to enhance the quality of learning?
- how confident are in using technology in your training session?
- what are the barriers which prevent you from exploiting the benefits of technology in your approach to teaching, training and supporting apprentices?

When used effectively, EdTech can have a positive impact on the quality of education. In their book on enhancing teaching and learning through technology, Ingle and Duckworth (2013b) highlight how effective use of technology can offer a range of benefits, such as providing more '**SPACE**' (Table 3.9).

Table 3.9 'SPACE': the benefits of using EdTech in apprenticeship training

Sharing	• Technologies can help tutors and apprentices share information about learning quickly and easily, especially where the training provider may be operating nationally, and apprentices are studying at a distance.
	• The use of electronic portfolios can help trainers, coaches and employers share information on the apprentice's progress, and their targets for development, helping to make meaningful links between on- and off-the-job training.
	• Using online video conferencing tools such as Zoom, Microsoft Teams and Google Meet can help the coach and learner to share their screen to talk about a presentation, to review feedback on specific parts of an assignment, or to walk through a particular website or learning resource together.
Personalisation	• Learning technologies can help to personalise the learning experience outside of the classroom, to ensure optimal challenge. For example, where some apprentices need additional support, trainers can direct them to complete self-directed e-learning modules to develop the foundation knowledge they need.

	• Trainers can use technologies to extend learning before and after a training session, for example setting flipped learning activities that should be completed online before the session, or home-learning activities that challenge apprentices to apply their learning from the session, or to go further with specific research activities after the session. • Trainers can signpost apprentices to online resources that will target their specific skills gaps, such as the development of referencing skills, or knowledge-based modules that they need to work on.
Accessibility	• Learning technologies can help apprentices with specific needs to access their learning. For example, most mainstream operating systems and office programmes now have a whole range of accessibility options that can support learners with additional needs, for example resizing icons, adjusting text size and colour, subtitling video content, reading text aloud, voice to text translations, simplifying menus and minimising distractions.
Communication	• One of the great advantages of learning technologies is to facilitate communication between learners, tutors and employers, for example the use of video conferencing platforms which allow all stakeholders to attend the important tripartite progress review meetings. • VLEs and social media platforms make use of discussion boards, chat rooms, forums where learners can discuss their learning with others in real time or asynchronously. • Some video conferencing systems allow learners to be put into smaller breakout rooms which make online group work easier. Group messaging services facilitate regular communication between learners and tutors from mobile devices.
Engagement	• The use of learning technologies may be a useful way to promote engagement and participation from apprentices. The use of online forms, voting software and polls and interactive assessment tools can all help to engage learners and encourage them to take an active role in their learning, asking questions and making a contribution. • The use of low-tech options such as quick response (QR) codes can encourage learners to use their mobile devices to participate, follow weblinks and access resources.

Top EdTech tools

A huge range of free, and paid-for, EdTech tools are available for teachers, trainers and tutors to enhance the quality of education for their apprentices. Instructors should choose tools which help to facilitate the very best practice in training and instruction, rather than just as an entertaining add-on. Table 3.10 highlights some freely available, and easy-to-use, tech tools which may be helpful for on- or off-the-job training, online, face-to-face or blended learning.

Table 3.10 EdTech tools

Tech tool	Pedagogical approach?	Application
iDocCam www.ipevo.com/ software	Modelling	Turn your smartphone into a visualiser with this free software. Share your screen to show learners how you work through a guided, worked example by hand, before they try it for themselves. For example, work through a maths problem or draw a diagram and flow chart, talking through each process and stage.
Google Docs and Jamboard docs.google.com jamboard.google.com	Cooperative learning	Set up an online document and share the links with apprentices to work in cooperative collaboration groups. This could be on a document, presentation or the Google Jamboard digital whiteboard. Assign an appropriate team leader to keep the group to time and focused on the task.
MindMeister www.mindmeister.com	Mapping	Create an online mindmap in minutes, individually or collaborating online with others. Highlight key concepts and the links between them, group ideas and show relationships and interdependencies.
Screen Capture www.loom.com screencast-o-matic.com	Present new information using small steps	Free screen capture software allows you to record a brief video clip of what's on your screen. This could be presentation slides, an article or a website for example. Make the clip available for apprentices to watch before a training session, so they are well prepared to ask questions, discuss and apply the material in the session.
	Summarising	Consider using a framework so learners do more than just watch the clip. Add additional requirements so they are active and generating learning, for example the '**WSQ**' approach developed by Crystal Kirch (@crystalkirch): (1) **Watch** - learners watch the clip and take notes (2) **Summarise** - learners select and organise their notes to provide a concise summary of the main learning points (3) **Question** - learners choose a question they have about the clip to bring to the session, for example something they were confused about or something to discuss in more detail.

Tech tool	Pedagogical approach?	Application
Nearpod www.nearpod.com	Guided practice Check for understanding	Nearpod allows tutors to deliver an interactive lesson containing a presentation, quizzes, polls and videos. The lesson can be student-paced (asynchronous) or trainer-led (synchronous), as learners log in to the website or app using a unique code.
Padlet www.padlet.com	Teaching Self-explaining Collaborative learning	Padlet is a digital noticeboard where learners can paste text, links, images and multimedia files. It can be used individually or as a group who have access via a weblink. Learners could be encouraged to complete a reflective task to summarise a key topic, explain their approach to a learning task or to teach other members of the group about a specific idea. Trainers can monitor contributions either synchronously or as a task set over a given time frame. Learners can comment on and critique their peers' responses or offer a counter-argument, for example.

These are just a few of the many tech tools which may add value to your training and provide opportunities for your learners to actively engage in the construction of their learning, not just as passengers watching tutors present content to them. We will explore more tech tools in the next chapter which explores ongoing assessment.

Trainers must take care, however, to ensure that their apprentices have access to the digital devices and internet connectivity they need, in order to be able to access online learning. In a JISC survey (2020) of further education (FE) learners, 32 per cent weren't able to say they had access to reliable WiFi, and 3 per cent said they didn't have access to a digital device at all (smartphone, laptop, desktop computer or tablet). Some learners may be in a household where they are sharing a digital device and to carry out their learning, they may need to use it at a quieter time, when there is less demand from others and the internet connection is not competing with streaming music or TV programmes, for example.

Key considerations for technology enhanced learning

- Consider the 'digital divide' – do all your apprentices have access to a reliable digital device and the internet connectivity they need to access e-learning materials? Can they loan equipment?

- Consider making hard-copy materials available for some learners – extracts of textbooks, case studies, PDFs, assignments.

- Not all learners may have easy access to a computer with a working camera and microphone and high-speed internet access to take part in a live (synchronous) online lesson at a set time. Consider making recordings available that they can access at a different time.

- Explore 'low tech' options that can be accessed on a smartphone over data connections. Use mobile applications (apps) such as CamScanner, to take photos of resources and easily convert them into a portable document format (PDF) to be stored and shared in an online folder such as Google Drive, Microsoft OneDrive or Dropbox.

- Think about the digital skills of apprentices – choose EdTech tools which are intuitive and easy to use. Avoid too many different tools and platforms which could be confusing and add to the learners' cognitive load.

Communicating and training online

As more and more learning moves onto an online environment, it is important to consider some of the training tools and techniques that can be important when you don't have the learners in front of you in a classroom. When using a video conferencing platform to deliver training sessions, get confident with the different tools and functions they have available, so you can use these to enhance delivery and promote effective learning.

- Set clear expectations for the curriculum to be covered – let apprentices know what you will be covering and when and how you will be approaching this. Get apprentices into a routine so they are familiar with your approach and the high expectations you have for participation and engagement.

- Email, or post on the VLE, pre-session activities to engage your apprentices before a live training session. This will be helpful to activate their prior knowledge and engage them in knowledge content before the session, so you can use the time to question, clarify, discuss and extend their learning.

- Call on learners throughout the session so they participate fully, either verbally or in the text chat box. Ask questions, check their understanding and encourage them to apply theory to their practical work context.

- Use the different functions of the platform you are using to best effect. For example, use breakout rooms to put apprentices in smaller groups where they can discuss, debate and work on a collaborative task. Use the polling feature at the start of a session to promote recall and active prior knowledge. Use the screenshare option for modelling and guiding learners through a process, sequence or method.

- Beware of 'zoombombing' – keep live online lessons secure, use passwords and the 'waiting room' feature, and don't make links public. Follow your institution's policy on social media and online/email communication with learners.

- Define clear boundaries for your working hours online and which methods of communication are appropriate. Consider having a 'virtual drop-in' time where any apprentice knows they can reach you online to ask a question, check their progress or clarify any misunderstandings.

- Minimise any distractions by clearing up your desktop icons, turning off notifications, checking your settings before the session. Be careful when sharing your screen, files or applications to ensure that data protection is not compromised.

- Track learning output rather than 'hours spent online'. Set clear milestones and deadlines, particularly for self-paced e-learning modules. Make the learning 'visible' for maximum accountability. For example, rather than just asking learners to work their way through online material, set generative learning tasks which help them to consolidate their learning into the long-term memory.

Next steps

Having explored different theories, models and tools of learning, do you think you might make any changes to the way you approach training apprentices, in groups or through one-to-one session, online or face-to-face? Think about the following **RIGGER** approach, which may help to structure an effective learning session for all apprentices (Figure 3.7):

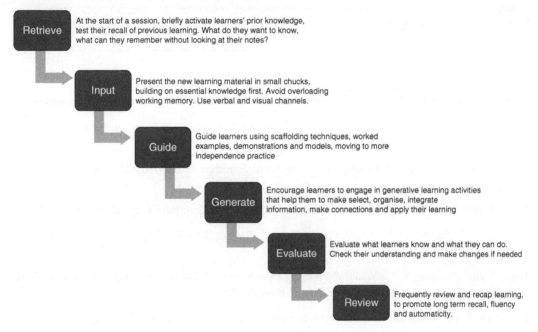

Figure 3.7 'RIGGER' – a structured approach to apprenticeship learning

A summary of key points

In this chapter we have looked at a number of key themes:

- choosing evidence-informed teaching strategies and approaches that lead to good learning, not just busy learners

- how educators and employers can work together to deliver on- and off-the-job training that complements and builds on each other

- the importance of getting the level of learning just right, so we challenge apprentices appropriately, without overloading their working memory and current capabilities

- how EdTech tools can be used when appropriate to enhance learning.

Key links

The Learning Scientists www.learningscientists.org	Free resources to help instructors prioritise training approaches that may be most effective.
Education and Training Foundation www.et-foundation.co.uk	Resources, courses and support for apprenticeship tutors, trainers and instructors, including EdTech and embedding English and maths.
JISC www.jisc.ac.uk/learning-and-research-resources	Learning and research resources that support vocational trainers' the use of EdTech and digital learning approaches.

▬ FURTHER READING ▬

Busch, B. and Watson, E. (2019) *The Science of Learning: 77 Studies That Every Teacher Needs to Know.* New York, NY: Routledge.

Didau, D. (2016) *What If Everything You Knew About Education Was Wrong?.* Wales: Crown House Publishing.

Enser, Z. and Enser, Z. (2020) *Generative Learning in Action.* London: John Catt Educational Limited.

Ingle, S. and Duckworth, V. (2013a) *Teaching and Training Vocational Learners.* Los Angeles, CA: Learning Matters.

Ingle, S. and Duckworth, V. (2013b) *Enhancing Learning Through Technology in Lifelong Learning: Fresh Ideas; Innovative Strategies.* Maidenhead: Open University Press.

Kirschner, P. and Hendrick, C. (2020) *How Learning Happens.* New York, NY: Routledge.

Lovell, O. (2020) *Cognitive Load Theory in Action.* Melton: John Catt Educational Limited.

Petty, G. (2006) *Evidence Based Teaching: A Practical Approach.* Cheltenham: Nelson Thornes.

Scott, D. (2018) *Learning Technology: A Handbook for FE Teachers and Assessors.* St Albans: Critical Publishing.

Sherrington, T. (2019) *Rosenshine's Principles in Action.* Melton: John Catt Educational Limited.

Weinstein, Y. and Sumeracki, M. (2019) *Understanding How We Learn: A Visual Guide.* New York, NY: Routledge.

4
ONGOING ASSESSMENT FOR VOCATIONAL LEARNERS

Feedback should be more work for the recipient than the donor.

Professor Dylan Wiliam

⌐ IN THIS CHAPTER ¬

In this chapter you will learn about:

- different types of assessment and feedback and when to use them
- approaches to questioning and practical ideas for the retrieval of learning
- different examples of education technologies to support ongoing, formative assessment
- preparing apprentices for their end-point assessments (EPAs) and achieving high grades
- how an understanding of different types of mistakes can help learning

This chapter has the following links to the assessor-coach apprenticeship standard (level 4):

Skills: the assessor-coach will be able to:	Knowledge: the assessor-coach will understand:
S2　apply or reference relevant initial and diagnostic assessment	K2　relevant forms of assessment to identify individual needs
S4　liaise with employers, colleagues and others to support learners' development	K4　additional support for learners available through workplace and provider-based colleagues
S7　give timely feedback on progress towards mastery of relevant skills and knowledge	K7　effective practice in giving feedback to guide progress and achievement

(Continued)

(Continued)

Skills: the assessor-coach will be able to:	Knowledge: the assessor-coach will understand:
S9 promote the safe and effective use of digital and mobile technologies to support learners and the assessor-coach role	K9 current and emerging technologies that could safely and effectively support learner autonomy and the assessor-coach role
S11 use effective listening, assertiveness and questioning to support learners' to engage with their learning plans and with assessment criteria and processes	K11 the effective use of active listening, assertiveness and questioning skills to support retention, progress and achievement

As we explored in the previous chapters, good apprenticeship teaching must be based on a clear and secure understanding of where our apprentices are now, where they need to be and how we can help them to get there. To do this, we need to use effective assessment. Let's remind ourselves of the apprenticeship journey and the use of different stages of assessment to ensure apprentices make great progress and can progress to their next steps.

Types of assessment

Initial and diagnostic assessment

Initial assessment is the process of assessing individual apprentices' starting points, their prior learning, current abilities and aptitudes. A number of paper-based and online tools can help trainers and coaches gather initial assessment information about their apprentices in order to plan an appropriate programme of on- and off-the-job training. Initial assessments are likely to cover existing vocational knowledge, skills and experience, English and maths skills, and readiness to learn.

Diagnostic assessment assesses more specifically what the learner already knows and the nature of any specific difficulties, gaps or challenges that they might have, which, if undiagnosed, might limit their progress and engagement. Diagnostic tools may be used to identify priorities in learning which require more input, support and focus, for example aspects of English and maths which require development. The outcomes of initial and diagnostic assessments are used to inform the individual learning plan (ILP) for the apprentice, in partnership with the employer.

Formative, ongoing assessment

Formative assessment is the ongoing process of continual monitoring to ensure that the learning plan is effective, supporting the apprentice to make good progress in the development of their knowledge, skills and workplace behaviours. As we explored in Chapter 3, Rosenshine's principles of instruction highlighted the importance of regular assessment, such as daily, weekly and monthly reviews of learning, the need to ask lots of questions, and to frequently check for learner understanding. This ongoing assessment can take many forms, and does not always have to be carried out by the trainer or coach. For example:

- **Tutor-led assessment:** where you as the trainer or coach make judgements on the level of learners' performance and their competence

- **Self-assessment:** where apprentices make their own judgement on their own levels of attainment

- **Peer-assessment:** where learners make assessment judgements on each other

- **Computer-based assessments:** for example, automated on-screen tests and quizzes which check learners' responses against the programmed correct answers

Trainers and coaches may choose to use a blend of ongoing assessment methods and types depending on the situation and context, such as whether you are assessing an individual or group of apprentices, or if you are assessing remotely at a distance or face-to-face. A broad range of different formative assessment tools are available to help assess apprentices' current level of competence. Some may be more suited to assessing knowledge, and others for assessing practical and technical skills or workplace behaviours. For example:

- questioning

- essays and formal written reports

- observation of skills and professional practice

- work-based projects

- tests, quizzes, polls and surveys

- individual, paired or group presentations

- reflective logs and professional journals

- portfolios and electronic portfolios (ePortfolios)

Assessment for learning

The outcomes of ongoing, formative assessments provide instructors, trainers, coaches and employers with invaluable feedback to find out which learning approaches, strategies and resources are working and where amendments and adaptations are needed. The outcomes of formative assessments also provide apprentices with the data they need to know how they are going and what they need to do next to keep making progress. Formative assessments help all apprenticeship stakeholders to identify when the apprentice is ready to proceed through the gateway and to the EPA process.

However, assessment should not be driving purpose for how apprenticeships are delivered. It is all too easy for tutors and trainers to get so focused on apprentices producing and recording evidence for audit and funding reasons, that the purposes of formative assessment are lost. Ongoing assessments should be used as a snapshot, to gain data on what apprentices know and can do, as a springboard to set challenging targets, and to inform the next steps of the programme. Training sessions and progress reviews should be about moving the apprentice forward, consolidating strengths, nurturing areas for development, practising and applying skills. Assessment records should capture this learning journey and the development of substantial new knowledge, skills and behaviours. However, completion of assessment tasks and paperwork should not be the main objective of these sessions.

Summative, end-point assessment

Summative assessment demonstrates the extent of apprentices' success in meeting the employer-designed occupational standard. In this respect, summative assessment is 'assessment *of* learning'. It is conducted through a process of EPA, which is unique to each standard, and outlined in the assessment plan for each standard. As we explored in Chapter 1, EPAs can take different forms such as observation of professional practice, professional discussion, formal tests and presentation of a portfolio of evidence. EPA is carried out by an appropriately experienced and qualified independent end-point assessor, to ensure the validity and reliability of the assessment. This is particularly important, as it is the achievement of the EPA that formally signals to employers that the apprentice is operating at or above the expected level of occupational competency for their role. Most EPAs have grading levels, such as pass, merit or distinction, that indicate the level of competency demonstrated.

Figure 4.1 highlights the different stages of assessment at different stages of the apprenticeship journey:

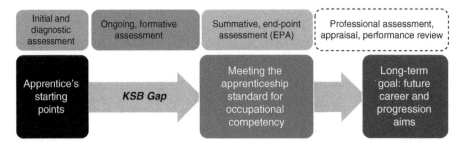

Figure 4.1 Stages of apprenticeship assessment

The road to mastery

In the previous chapter, we explored effective ways of teaching and instructing and the need to activate apprentices in generative learning processes. This helps them to select, organise and integrate new information, make connections, develop understanding and meaning. In order for apprentices to use this new insight, they need to store and remember this new learning in their long-term memory, but also be able to retrieve it quickly and easily when they need it, for example when they are in the workplace or their EPA. Through repeated practice and application, apprentices begin to become more secure in their knowledge, more confident in their skills, and develop greater speed, accuracy and fluency.

Think about when learning how to ride a bike or drive a car. The first few attempts seem like an almost impossible task. You fall off, you stall, you might get angry and upset, but through a combination of instruction, coaching, assessment and feedback, persistence and practice, these skills are mastered. Some take longer than others, some need more feedback and coaching, some need more time to practise their skills. Over time, these skills become so fluent that they almost become automatic. You can do them almost without thinking, freeing up your working memory to take on board new or more complex skills and challenges. But how do we get novice apprentices to this point of mastery and automaticity?

Retrieve to remember

Following a training session, apprentices may appear to have mastered the new material; they can often answer questions about what they have just covered and may have taken lots of detailed notes. However, research tells us that most students will quickly forget much of what has been learnt only once, so when it gets to the time of the exam, test or EPA, apprentices we thought had the content mastered, might not do so well. So what are the implications for trainers and the approach to assessment?

Psychologist Hermann Ebbinghaous (1885) is probably best known for his studies on memory and forgetting. His experiments and studies showed that although we are likely to quickly forget large amounts of knowledge that we have encountered once, if we encounter the material again and again, the rate at which we forget reduces over time. Therefore, it's a good idea if we regularly return to previously learnt material, to test how much our learners can remember, then recap, revise and build on that content, rather than just teach it once and move on. This way, we get our learners working hard to commit the knowledge to their long-term memory.

As well as getting the new material into our learners' memory, we also need to get it out again. This is important so they can demonstrate what they know and can do at work, perform well in their occupation roles, and do well in those all-important EPAs and Functional Skills exams! This is where retrieval practice (sometimes known as the testing effect) comes in; getting learners to practise retrieving knowledge from their long-term memories, through quizzes and tests. This will help to ensure that learning sticks over the long term.

Making memories

Spend a few minutes at the start of each training session to review previous learning, to test what apprentices can remember or do. This is a great way to slow the curve of forgetting, and strengthen learning over time. Learners should avoid using any notes they have taken but instead, complete activities which activate their long-term memory and test what they can retrieve. This could be as simple as asking a few questions or prompts based on material covered in previous sessions, for example:

- **3-2-1:** identify **three** key things that we covered last lesson, describe **two** ways the things we learnt can be used in your workplace, ask **one** question about something you are confused about or would like to know more about.

- **On the job:** discuss with a partner, one way you have applied what we learnt two sessions ago in your role at work.

- **Memory master:** Without looking at your notes, spend 3 minutes writing everything you can remember about what we covered in our session 3 weeks ago.

- **Picture it:** you have 5 minutes to create a diagram or image that reflects what we have studied so far in this module. Use key words and connections to make relevant links.

Increase the space between revision and retrieval activities, to gradually test the knowledge and material that was covered further and further back in the learning programme. Figure 4.2 provides an example of a possible retrieval practice grid for hospitality team member (food and beverage service) apprentices.

FIND OUT MORE

In her popular book on retrieval practice (2019), Kate Jones provides a range of practical ideas to consider using as part of the retrieval practice part of a training or review session. For example, challenge grids can encourage and motivate learners to retrieve knowledge learnt in previous sessions. For more information visit: www.lovetoteach87.com

State the core temperature for a joint of meat during service	State **two** examples of workplace legislation	Explain **two** principles of silver service	Give **three** examples of internal customers
State **two** ways to minimise waste	Explain **one** benefit of using local suppliers	State the next action after providing diners with menus	Demonstrate **one** example of positive body language
How long can cold food be left on display before disposal?	Give **two** reasons for efficient resource use	Describe the correct place for wine glasses for formal dinner service	Identify the first action in dealing with a complaint
Describe **two** environmental controls that need to be checked	Provide a definition of hospitality	Give **one** example of an imperial measurement found in hospitality	Explain **three** reasons for having brand standards
Last session (1)	*Two weeks ago (2)*	*A month ago (3)*	*Further back (4)*

Figure 4.2 Retrieval practice challenge grid (inspired from an idea by Kate Jones (@87History))

When apprentices have had some initial instruction in a given topic or area, consider interleaving and interweaving related, but different topics into the sequence of learning, rather than in one mass block. Whilst this may initially seem confusing to learners, interleaving content from different topic areas has shown to have a positive impact on learning in the long term. Interleaving also builds in space between different topics, modules and units, allowing trainers to test and assess the content that was covered a few sessions or weeks ago.

For example, a vocational skills trainer working with apprentice commis chefs might initially teach basic preparation and cooking skills such as weighing, measuring, sieving, mixing, steaming and frying but then interleave different skills and activities for pastry, bread, cake, cold and hot desserts, rather than teaching each skill individually in a block, before moving on to the next area. This way of organising the curriculum may seem quite 'messy' but could be a much more effective way of developing apprentices' secure knowledge and skills over the long term.

Make difficulty desirable

Many learners will feel successful if they are able to complete a quiz or skills assessment quickly and easily. However, it is the challenging mental effort that makes testing and retrieval activities so helpful for learning, remembering and strengthening the mental connections that learning has created. Learners shouldn't be able to use their notes simply to 'find' the information, they need to work hard and think hard to recall and retrieve the information from their long-term memory.

When this becomes easy, it may be time to make the test or activity more difficult, so learners have to struggle. Although it may not feel like it to the apprentice, this increased difficulty is actually very welcome, as it helps the learner to become secure in their knowledge and skills, being able to remember more and do more. This notion of 'desirable difficulties' is a term coined by Professor Robert Bjork (1994) to explain the value in varying the conditions of learning, to make it less predictable, and more challenging, in order to enhance learning and make it more flexible and durable over time.

Interleaving different topics of study, rather than as a massed block, is one way to increase the level of difficulty. Adding space between the testing of topics is also another useful way to increase the level of challenge and difficulty and the impact on learning over time. Another possibility to consider is varying the conditions of study. Research has shown that when the learning takes place in more varied and less predictable environments and contexts, this can lead to an improvement in learning and retrieval. So, for example, apprentices who always carry out retrieval practice exercises in the spare room at home for an upcoming test might not be as effective as learners who revise in the spare room, in the staff room at work and on the train home after work.

FIND OUT MORE

Watch this short clip from Professors Elizabeth and Robert Bjork on desirable difficulties and think how you could apply the four desirable difficulties in your practice.

www.apprenticeships.today/difficulties

Find some time to talk to apprentices about how they learn and remember, so they understand how best to approach their studies and preparation from summative assessments. When revising for a test or exam, most apprentices may think that re-reading their notes and 'cramming' are effective strategies. However, the research tells us these strategies are usually much less effective at retaining what we have learnt in the long term, although they may give the illusion of knowing and a false sense of security.

REFLECTION POINT

Using retrieval activities, tests and quizzes without looking at notes is clearly more difficult for learners that simply re-reading their notes taken in training sessions many times. Trainers and coaches need to be careful not to make learning too difficult too soon, however, or this may send the apprentice into the 'panic zone', increase anxiety and switch them off from the learning.

Trainers, coaches and employers know their apprentices best. Training is a skilled profession and getting the level of challenge and difficulty just right will need to be carefully balanced to really maximise learning and progress. Frequent ongoing assessments are an essential way of getting the data needed to get this balance right.

- How might you encourage your learners to use more testing as a way to boost their learning and knowledge retention over time, even when they may get low scores at first and find this difficult?

- Do you feel using more testing would be helpful to try and reduce learners' test anxiety as they become more familiar with the process and responding to the outcomes?

Questioning is key

As we explored in Chapter 3, the importance of effective questioning cannot be overstated when helping apprentices to learn and remember. Using a range of different question types and questioning techniques can help apprentices to develop a secure understanding of the knowledge and skills they need.

Closed questions

Closed questions can be answered with a single definitive response, for example yes or no, true or false. These types of questions can be useful for quickly testing factual knowledge that often have a one word or short answer. As the answer is often definitive, closed questions are often used in automated quizzes and tests. Examples of closed questions are as follows:

- Clinic waste must be disposed of in which colour bag?

- Who is the authority responsible for enforcing the Health and Safety at Work Act 1974?

- Retailers are not permitted by law to sell solvents to people under what age?

- Do you understand what we have just covered?

- Are you clear on what you have to do?

The last two questions in that list demonstrate some of the clear limitations of closed questions. Learners may frequently answer with a confident 'yes' but it may not be clear that they do have a secure understanding and therefore additional checks on learning will be needed.

Open questions

Open questions require a more free-form, extended answer that cannot be answered with a simple yes or no. Open questions are usually more effective at drawing out learners' thoughts, perceptions, understanding and opinions than closed questions, which promote a specific, set or limited response. Open questions can be useful to promote thinking and reasoning, to assess how well an apprentice understands something, the depth of their knowledge, if they understand why they are performing a particular skill, or using a specific tool for example. Examples of open questions are as follows:

• Tell me why it is important for a health-care assistant to establish consent for an activity or action?

• Explain why you have chosen that particular tool to carry out that job?

• How should a driver deal with an emergency situation onboard their bus?

• How can you identify if electrical tools are fit for purpose?

• How have you use your knowledge of leadership styles in your role at work?

• How might you research for the information you need for your work project?

• If you come up against barriers in your learning, what actions could you take to overcome them?

General or nominated?

General questions are often asked verbally to a whole group of apprentices. They can be a useful way to explore learners' prior knowledge on a particular topic as learners volunteer to answer and make a contribution. Whist this avoids putting anyone 'on the spot', it can often lead to a few learners dominating the answers. It can also give trainers a false sense of the current level of understanding in the room, as those who are less confident may try and avoid participating. Open or closed questions can be asked in a general way, for example:

• Who can tell me anything about the circulatory system?

• Does anyone know how the General Data Protection Regulations affect their organisation?

• What are the common weaknesses in a small organisations' IT security systems?

Unlike general questions, nominated, directed or targeted questioning is aimed at a specific learner. This allows the trainer to assess their particular level of knowledge and understanding. Learners who lack confidence in their abilities, or who feel they may look silly or stupid for offering an incorrect answer, may find this style of questioning challenging. Rather than losing the clear benefits of a targeted questioning approach, tutors, trainers and coaches should aim to quickly establish a learning environment of mutual trust and respect, a safe space where apprentices understand the value of having a go, participating and learning from mistakes. We will explore apprentices' beliefs about learning in the next chapter. Examples of nominated questions are as follows:

- Trudy, please tell me, what information must the dispensing label on prescription medication include?

- Darshak, what are the differences between fixed and variable costs?

Rather than nominating the specific learner before the question is asked, it may be more effective to pose the question first, pause and then select the learner to ask. This may help to ensure all learners pay attention, as the question may be coming their way! If the learner's name is stated before the question, some learners may tune out as they know they are not being assessed. For example:

- What is the difference between a risk and a hazard... Christian?

- How can we demonstrate professionalism in our role at work... Flora?

- What would be an example of non-verbal communication... Mandy?

FIND OUT MORE

In his book Teach Like a Champion (2015) teacher, trainer and author Doug Lemov outlines the benefits of the 'Cold Call' questioning technique, where students are selected after the question has been posed and a period of thinking, or 'wait time' has been given. This approach means you can assess every learner, not just those volunteering to answer, and it creates a culture of accountability, where all are expected to listen and participate. For more information and resources, why not explore: www.teachlikeachampion.com/resources

Probing, funnelling and differentiated questions

Probing questions can help trainers to assess learners' level and depth of understanding by asking a number of follow-up questions. Probing questions might require learners to provide a specific example, their own viewpoint and opinion, or a reason or justification. Skillful probing questioning can help learners to develop more meaning and insight into a particular topic or concept. A funnelling approach to questioning can start with some straightforward closed questions which continue to broaden into more detailed, in-depth open questions. This can be a useful approach to get less confident learners engaged in the line of questions, for example:

1. Who can give me an example of a specific need that a customer may have... Melanie?

2. How could a hotel make reasonable adjustments for their visual impairment?

3. What legislation protects the rights of those with a disability?

4. What might be the implications for the hotel if reasonable adjustments are not made?

5. Can you give me a specific example of how your business meets the needs of customers with a different disability?

6. How do you feel when you are helping a customer with a specific need you are less confident about?

7. Where could you get support in order to develop your skills and confidence further?

TAKE IT FURTHER

The 'Pose – Pause – Pounce – Bounce' questioning technique takes the Cold Call approach one step further by following up the first question with an extension or probing question aimed at another learner in the group.

Step 1:	Pose the question – ensure all learners are focused and listening
Step 2:	Pause – give all learners some thinking/wait time
Step 3:	Pounce – nominate a specific learner to offer a response; they may need a clue or prompt if appropriate
Step 4:	Bounce – extend the question or response by moving to another learner in the group. Can they add to or challenge the first response, can they go deeper, can they provide an example, what is their view?

FIND OUT MORE

How much thinking (or wait) time should we give learners to answer a question before 'pouncing' for a response? Studies have shown (Rowe, 1986) that teachers and trainers typically wait less than a second after asking a question for their learners to reply. After the learner stops speaking, tutors typically wait less than a second before beginning their response of clarification or asking their next question. The study demonstrated that if tutors and trainers can increase the wait time to 3 seconds in both cases, the number and length of student responses increased significantly.

REFLECTION POINT

- Are you conscious about how much wait time you leave after asking a question? Do you worry about periods of silence or disruptive behaviour if you leave time for thinking?

- Are you worried about putting apprentices on the spot and making them feel embarrassed or silly if they don't quickly have the answer?

- What could you do to make your use of questioning more effective?

Depending on apprentices' current level of skills and expertise, questions can be pitched and differentiated accordingly to ensure they require learners to think hard, but are not so challenging or straightforward that learners move into the panic or coasting zone, as we explored in Chapter 3. If learners are easily getting all questions correct, we may need to increase the level of challenge with more complex, open and probing questions which require examples, clarification and reasoning.

Careful correction

If apprentices are unable to answer a question correctly, trainers and coaches should be careful not to rush in too quickly and provide immediate correction and the right answer. Apprentices may need a little more support, but to develop their skills, confidence, independence, the right type of 'nudge' should be used at the right time. Table 4.1 explores different responses that trainers could take, following questioning or another type of assessment, if learners are not quite there yet.

Table 4.1 Scaffolding framework

1. Correcting	Correction is a direct intervention and one which may be necessary if the apprentice could harm themselves or others, or cause significant disruption or damage if they were to get something wrong.	An advanced beauty therapy apprentice may be carrying out a massage to increase lymphatic drainage of their client. During questioning and an observation assessment, the trainer identifies that the apprentice is not clear about the correct technique to use and they may need to step in to correct them.
2. Modelling	If assessment identifies that the apprentice is struggling to master a new skill, the trainer or workplace supervisor can help by modelling again how to carry out a particular task, process or procedure. The apprentice can then try this again themselves with supervision, practising frequently as required to build confidence, fluency and automaticity.	Following assessment in the salon, it is clear that an apprentice barber is struggling to perfect their razor cutting technique to get the neckline shape their clients want. The skills trainer can provide additional modelling to help the apprentice understand the different techniques, followed by additional practice.
3. Clueing	As the apprentice becomes more skilled, direct modelling and demonstration will no longer be required but some learners may need a clue to keep them on the right track.	Following an assessment at work, a business administration apprentice might need a clue that the icon they are looking for is on the top ribbon menu, or they may need a clue on how to review the paper settings before sending a document to print.

4. Prompting	An apprentice may have a good idea about what they need to do but lacks confidence to get started. They may respond well to a small prompt or nudge from the trainer to get them started and to inspire confidence that they are on the right track.	A Functional Skills tutor might provide some positive prompting to an apprentice preparing for their speaking and listening assessment, be asking them what their presentation topic is about, how they researched their topic and what questions they think might be asked.
5. Self-scaffolding	Hopefully apprentices will develop the confidence and independence to know what to do when they don't know the answer to a question or are struggling to perform a skill correctly. Learners may get to the point where they should be able to draw on resources and take actions needed to close their own knowledge gaps.	During a training session, an apprentice's early years practitioner realises that he knows very few of the questions posed at the start of the lesson, which is a recap of things they have covered earlier in the course. He sets a plan to go back and summarise his notes using the Cornell system, and then use a quizzing app to test his own knowledge each week.

(Adapted from Bosanquet, Radford, & Webster, 2016)

Peer and self-assessment

As well as trainers and coaches implementing all the assessments, apprentices can be encouraged to assess themselves and each other. Peer and self-assessment techniques can be effective in helping learners to retrieve and consolidate previously learnt information. In her book *Making Good Progress* (2016), educator and author Daisy Christodoulou highlights how being able to tell the difference between competence and incompetence is an aspect of developing competence. So, developing our learners' skills and abilities involves developing their ability to perceive quality; to know what's effective, what meets professional standards and what needs improvement.

Helping apprentices to understand what makes a piece of work high quality will help them to make judgements on the quality of their own work, and that of their peers and colleagues. Being able to identify improvements will help them to identify where they need to be and what they need to do to close this gap, make progress and achieve or exceed a minimum level of occupational competency. Making time for learners to engage in a process of self- or peer assessment, therefore, can be a useful way to try and develop their competency, rather than the trainer or coach making all the judgements.

Think, pair, square, share

This popular technique encourages learners to think about a question or problem individually, where they then compare their answers and thoughts with a partner. They can be encouraged to explore similarities and difference in their responses, debate if someone is right or wrong if the answers are different, explore which response best fits the question or task. The pair can then be encouraged to square their findings with others in their group or on their table. This widens the debate to a greater

Figure 4.3 Think, pair, square, share

range of ideas and responses, which could be quite different or there may be a useful consensus of opinion. Finally, each group is asked to share their findings to explore the level of knowledge and understanding in the room (Figure 4.3).

Care should be taken to monitor self- and peer assessment activities to ensure that accurate and useful feedback is being provided. Professor Graham Nuthall's (2007) studies into the 'hidden lives of learners' identified that as much as 80 per cent of feedback learners receive from their peers was inaccurate in a classroom environment. The trainer's role of checking for understanding is still therefore essential. Learners may struggle to assess, and provide useful feedback, to their peers based on the quality of their work. There could be a reluctance to be 'critical' of others in the group for fear of upsetting friends and colleagues.

Learners may need some support in understanding how to carry out effective peer assessment and how to provide feedback which is both supportive and helpful. Learners should be encouraged to see constructive feedback as desirable, as it is offered to help them improve and progress. All apprentices should be prepared to step up to give specific and helpful feedback and also to take on board the feedback given by others, including workplace mentors and supervisors. The following constructive 'feedback starters' may be helpful for learners when beginning to provide peer feedback:

- Your second paragraph on management theories could be better explained if you...

- Your furniture making drawing was not fully accurate as...

- I though the way you dealt with that customer complaint was really effective because...

- Section three in your showcase portfolio would demonstrate your technical skills more clearly if you include...

- Your free-hand cutting of the construction materials would be easier if you...

Fantastic feedback

Well done, great job, good work, excellent. Whilst praise statements like these are quick and easy to write, they do not represent effective feedback as they provide no information to guide learners' future behaviour, unlike the more specific peer feedback prompts above. Researchers are agreed that providing effective feedback can have a significant impact on learning, progress and achievement. However, studies have also shown that the quality of feedback provided by teachers and trainers varies significantly, so how we give feedback is important.

In their article on the power of feedback, Hattie and Timperly (2007) explore different feedback perspectives, uses and types. It is useful to consider three important questions (Table 4.2).

Table 4.2 Three feedback questions

1. Where am I going? 'Feed-up'	Do your apprentices know what they need to know and do? Learners need to know and understand what their learning outcomes, objectives or goals are, in order to identify where they are now and the gap between the two. When learners are committed to achieving their goals, they are more likely to take onboard constructive feedback to help close the gap and achieve their goal. The goal, or target, should be focused on the specific knowledge, skills or behaviours the apprentice needs to develop, rather than the completion of a specific task or activity. For example, an apprentice bricklayer might be working towards developing her skills in cutting and laying bricks to set dimensions and applying mortar with a trowel. The goal is not to 'pass the observation' or complete 'unit 2'. The feed-up might also relate to what the apprentice needs to do to achieve the distinction grade standard in their end-point assessment.
2. How am I going? 'Feed-back'	This is verbal or written feedback on the progress that the apprentice is making towards the goal. For example, following a practical observation assessment, the trainer will provide specific feedback to help the apprentice understand what they have done well and where improvements still need to be made. It helps trainers identify what additional teaching, demonstrating and modelling may be required for the learner to move forward. For example, the apprentice may be struggling to shape and trim bricks to size effectively using a hammer and chisel.
3. Where to next? 'Feed-forward'	Trainers and coaches can provide advice and guidance to apprentices on what they might need to do next to make better progress. This could be more time spent deliberately practising a specific skill, observing the work of others, carrying out more research, completing online learning materials. For example, the vocational trainer may help the apprentice to identify they need to further develop their applied maths skills in order to calculate the number of bricks needed and work with different or undersized bricks.

(Based on Hattie & Timperly, 2007)

When providing feedback, most trainers often focus on the specific task being undertaken. Whilst this is important, particularly where the task is new learning, feedback can also focus on the learning processes, the approach, strategy or resources used by the learner when undertaking the task. Feedback can also focus on how well the learner is able to direct, manage and self-regulate their own learning, so they can become more independent over time, and less reliant on the trainer or coach. Table 4.3 explores the differences between the three different levels of feedback.

By providing apprentices with process, and self-regulation level feedback, we encourage them to develop effective learning habits that they can transfer to different aspects of their learning and their work. Feedback at the self-level, such as 'You did a great job, well done', provides the learner with no feedback to guide their future learning behaviours and should be avoided.

Table 4.3 Levels of feedback

Task level	Feedback on how well tasks are understood or performed.	Your presentation on team management does not demonstrate your knowledge of emotional intelligence. You need to cover this in more detail.
Process level	Feedback on the key process needed to understand or perform tasks.	Your use of Wikipedia to carry out your research did not produce the most valid and reliable information. You need to use a wider variety of good quality sources.
Self-regulation level	Feedback to inform self-monitoring, directing and regulating actions.	What could you do to develop your skills in carrying out effective online research from good quality sources?

(Adapted from Hattie & Timperly, 2007)

Assessment for learning expert Professor Dylan Wiliam (www.dylanwiliam.org) highlights a number of key goals that educators should strive for in providing feedback to learners:

- Feedback to learners should focus on what they need to do to improve, rather than on how well they have done

- Avoid telling students to work harder or be 'more systematic' – the feedback should contain a recipe for future action

- Feedback should be designed so as to lead all students to believe that ability is incremental

- Feedback should be more work for the recipient than the donor

- Don't give feedback unless you allocate class time for students to respond

- Feedback should avoid comparison with others. Students given marks are likely to see it as a way to compare themselves with others; those given only comments see it as helping them to improve. The latter group outperforms the former.

Time for DIRT

If tutors, trainers and coaches are going to spend precious time writing careful, constructive feedback to guide learners' future improvement, then time should be made in training sessions to allow apprentices to respond to that feedback. This is especially important for apprentices who are very busy at work and those who less likely to carry out much independent learning outside of the session. It may be helpful to build in some 'DIRT' to a training session (**D**edicated **I**mprovement and **R**eflection **T**ime), to provide learners with some protected time to respond to the improvements and actions highlighted in their feedback. In this way, the status and importance of the feedback is maintained, and the time spent by trainers and coaches providing it is more likely to have a positive impact.

No more marks?

Having assessed a piece of learner work such as quiz or test, it is very tempting to add up the scores and highlight a final mark, but what happens when the results are distributed to a group of learners? Much time is often spent comparing grades against one another – *'what did you get?'*. Having received the grade, there is often little need to access the detailed written feedback which highlights areas of the task requiring further improvement, or advice on key learning process to enhance to do better next time. The inclusion of the mark or grade removes the need to engage in the feedback in order for learners to work out how well they have done. In the formative stages of learning therefore, not including the mark might be an effective way of encouraging learners to engage more deeply in their feedback and by doing so, take on board the actions that will help them to progress even further. Marks could be released when learners have read and responded appropriately to their feedback, if appropriate.

REFLECTION POINT

- How do you check for understanding to be confident that apprentices have learnt what is required?

- Do you encourage peer assessment in your training sessions and what are the barriers to ensuring this is effective? How could you better prepare your learners to give specific and helpful feedback to their peers?

- Thinking about the feedback you give to your apprentices, do you provide task, process and self-regulation feedback where appropriate?

- Even though apprentices may like to hear it, what are some of the disadvantages of giving 'self-level' feedback to learners?

- Do you ever give feedback on marked work that includes an overall score or grade? What would happen if you didn't provide the mark, or you withheld the mark until learners had read and responded to their feedback first?

TAKE IT FURTHER

Following appropriate formative assessment, it may become clear that an apprentice needs to further develop their skills in a particular area. Rather than 'practice making perfect', practice makes *progress*. Psychologist K Anders Ericson is probably best known for his studies on expertise and 'deliberate practice'. Rather than just a process of naive repetition, or accumulating experience, to improve a particular skill, deliberate practice involves considerable, specific and sustained effort. Learners need to pinpoint a particular aspect of their role of skill they need to improve on. By spending time purposefully practising this skill in a focused and deliberate way, and receiving effective and specific feedback from a coach or trainer, learners can then put in the work needed to improve. When they have improved, new specific goals are set, and the process of deliberate practice continues.

For example, an apprentice sporting excellence professional footballer may need to develop his skills in manipulating and controlling the ball through headers. To hone these specific skills, it would be far more profitable to engage in deliberate practice in heading the ball, rather than playing full match after match, when there would be few chances to practise heading the ball. The apprentice should also receive precise feedback from their coach on how to develop their skills, so they can monitor their progress and accuracy as they work on their skills deliberately. Learners could also use technology to capture and analyse their performance by video. Once mastered, new goals can be set to extend the player's expertise in passing, or shooting the ball through headers.

Find out more by reading 'Peak: How All of Us Can Achieve Extraordinary' by Anders Ericsson and Robert Pool (2016).

Overlearning

When should apprentices stop practising their skills? There is a temptation to practise our skills to the point of mastery – when we can do it comfortably without support, and then move on. As we have already explored, however, over time, we may lose the ability to perform these skills quickly and easily when we need to. Overlearning is the process of continuing to practise a task or skill even when this has been mastered to some degree. This ongoing rehearsal and repetition can help to lock in the skills, so apprentices can perform them fluently, accurately, consistently, to a point where it also becomes automatic, or second nature. There may not be sufficient time in training sessions to allow for overlearning, so apprentices could be encouraged to continue practising and rehearing their skills in the workplace and through independent study, to further develop and secure their levels of competency.

CASE STUDY

Iqbal is a vocational skills trainer who works with a caseload of IT apprentices who work for different employers across the whole of England. Apprentices attend his training as part of a block, focussing on different modules at each visit, usually around one month apart. Although apprentices leave each block training week with a good understanding of the topics covered, Iqbal is aware that unless they are using and applying the knowledge and skills in the workplace straightaway, there is a good chance they will soon start to forget what they have covered by their next visit. He is mindful that they need to complete specific professional qualification tests as part of their apprenticeship and they need to have secure skills and clear understanding to pass.

Before apprentices attend their next block training week, Iqbal emails them a link to a questionnaire he has set up using Google Forms. Apprentices need to answer a variety of multiple choice, open and closed questions which tests their knowledge on topics previously covered. The questions get progressively more difficult and complex. At the end of the online form, there is a space for apprentices to complete a self-assessment of how they think they have done and any areas they feel are less secure. This ongoing assessment information helps Iqbal to tailor the training sessions to the needs of the group, or to support individual learners with their particular training needs, signposting additional resources or practice exercises if needed. Iqbal always provides verbal feedback to each apprentice during the block training week, as well as completing written feedback on the learner management system, which can be accessed by the learner, their skills coach and their employer.

This written feedback focuses on their learners' practical skills development and areas that need to be practised or developed further. The feedback helps the skills coaches to monitor areas for development and work with the employer to amend the work experience if necessary, for example identifying different duties and tasks they could take on at work so they can apply, practise and consolidate what they have learnt in their training sessions in a real-world setting.

REFLECTIVE QUESTIONS

- How could you use ongoing assessments to help your learners regularly retrieve the information they need?
- If the majority of learners struggled to retrieve the information from previous learning sessions, what actions would you take?

Preparing for end-point assessment

As we explored in earlier chapters, each apprenticeship standard has an EPA, except for a small number of professionally regulated standards where achievement is through an established professional competency test. One key aspect of ongoing, formative assessment and feedback is to ensure apprentices know what knowledge, skills and behaviours they need to develop and demonstrate in order to meet the higher grades threshold. This is not about preparing learners to 'pass the test' but having high expectations about what apprentices can do if they are to exceed the minimum levels of occupational competency set by the trailblazer group. If apprentices are not clear on what 'distinction standard' looks like, it will be difficult for them to close the gap between where they are now and where they want to be. Typically, higher grades are often awarded where apprentices:

- consistently demonstrate accurate application of skills and expertise
- are able to develop others as well as themselves
- are able to confidently justify their actions, decisions and choices
- demonstrate a thorough depth of understanding
- can provide a wide range of different examples and applications.

Trainers, coaches and employers should clearly understand the EPA arrangements for the standards they are involved in, and the level of competency required to achieve the high grades. The EPA assessment plan is a key document which outlines expectation at each level. These plans are interpreted by EPA awarding organisations and the independent end-point assessors. Ongoing assessment and feedback should also consider these standards to best inspire and motivate apprentices to progress beyond minimum expectations. Table 4.4 explores some of the requirements of different apprenticeships at pass and distinction standard.

Table 4.4 End point assessment requirements

Apprenticeship standard	Pass standard	Distinction standard
Plasterer (Level 2)	Plasterboard joints: 2 mm gap Plasterboard fixing centres: 300 mm ± 6 mm Fixings: less than 20% of fixings too deep or proud of the surface	Plasterboard joints: **less than** 2 mm gap Plasterboard fixing centres: 300 mm **± 3 mm** Fixings: **less than 10%** of fixings too deep or proud of the surface
Adult Care Worker (Level 2)	Apprentice is able to demonstrate that they can use verbal and non-verbal communication skills and techniques to communicate effectively with individuals, family members, carers or advocates.	Apprentice is able to demonstrate that they can take **appropriate actions** to communicate effectively with individuals in situations where there are environmental **barriers to communication.**
Business Administrator (Level 3)	Demonstrates they can use IT packages, specifically to write letters or emails, and to record and analyse information.	**Consistently** demonstrates they can use IT packages and can **provide varied, quality examples.**
Advanced Beauty Therapist (Level 3)	Explains the effects of different technology therapy equipment, their uses, restrictions and benefits when used individually or in combination to meet the client's needs.	**Justifies in technical detail** the treatment **rationale**, duration and sequence for the combinations or individual application of techniques to **maximise** and meet the treatment objectives.
Countryside Ranger (Level 4)	Describes and explains the main practical land and habitat management techniques used for a range of habitats and how to balance conflicting needs.	**Critically compares** the choice of practical and land management techniques with others that could have been selected.
Learning and Skills Teacher (Level 5)	Demonstrates how they ensure their vocational knowledge and skills are fully up-to-date with current practices within the workplace.	Demonstrates **expertise, passion** and **currency** that **enthuses** and **motivates** learners in the context of the subject being taught, and **exemplifies their expertise** based on **latest thinking**, personal experiences and the **range** of subject-specific tools and techniques.

REFLECTION POINT

- What formative assessment strategies would you carry out to help you understand the apprentice's current level of competence?

- How would you prepare apprentices to make the step up from the minimum level of occupational competency at the pass standard, to meet the distinction standard requirements?

- How would you deal with an apprentice who is happy to settle for meeting the minimum standards but you know they are capable of so much more?

- How confident are you with the assessment plan and EPAs of the standards that you are working with? How could you develop your knowledge and confidence with the summative assessment requirements further?

Technologies for assessment

We explored a range of 'EdTech' options for teaching and training in the last chapter. Learning technologies can also be useful when carrying out ongoing assessments of apprentice's knowledge, skills and behaviours. Smartphone apps, websites and virtual learning environment can all be used effectively to engage apprentices and to test their progress and current levels of skills competency and ability. Let's take a look at some of the popular options used by tutors, assessors and coaches, which all have useful free options, as well as additional paid-for functionality (Table 4.5).

Table 4.5 Top EdTech tools for ongoing assessment

Tech tool	What does it do?	Application ideas
Socrative www.socrative.com	Very popular with educators globally, Socrative provides a website and free mobile app where trainers can quickly and easily set apprentices quizzes, polls, competitions and surveys to test their learning and promote retrieval.	Luke is a hairdressing apprentice trainer. He sets his learners a weekly Socrative quiz as a retrieval practice activity based on theory content covered in previous sessions. He shares the room code and apprentices log in on their mobile phones. He tracks their scores each week and provides additional support to those who need it.
Flipgrid www.flipgrid.com	Almost like TikTok for learning! Flipgrid is a simple, free and accessible video discussion tool from Microsoft where apprentices can use their mobile digital devices to record a short video to respond	Sandi is an early years practitioner skills coach. She works with apprentices on a one-to-one basis across the whole county. She encourages her caseload of apprentices to record Flipgrid videos

(Continued)

Table 4.5(Continued)

Tech tool	What does it do?	Application ideas
	to a discussion or assessment topic set by the tutor. Other learners can log in, comment and take the discussion further.	based on her topic of the month, for example safeguarding, diversity and SEN. This helps her apprentices to feel part of a group and allows Sandi to monitor their developing knowledge and understanding, and correct any misunderstanding.
Thinglink www.thinglink.com	Thinglink allows trainers and learners to turn an image into an interactive graphic, adding text, images and multimedia. They can be shared online and make an engaging formative assessment activity for learners to create.	Nicki is a construction instructor. She sets her apprentices a task to create an interactive Thinglink by taking a photo of a building site that they are working on. Learners then add text, audio or video to different parts of the image, highlighting and explaining hazards and safety measures. They then email her the link so she can check on their progress any understanding.
Quizlet www.quizlet.com	Quizlet allows learners and trainers to create flashcard sets, or other study tools, to help them remember important knowledge and learning content. Learners can use the resources to practise retrieving the prompts, such as images and key words.	Selma is a training consultant working with business administration apprentices. Some of her apprentices struggle with the knowledge test of the EPA, so she uses Quizlet to set up flashcards which test the knowledge aspects of the standard. This helps her learners to practise before they get to the gateway.
Microsoft Forms forms.office.com	Create a quiz, poll or survey in minutes. Use a mix of multiple choice, short answer and long answer questions to check for learners' understanding. Easily analyse scores to identify where additional training or support is needed.	Pauline is an assessor-coach who supports business administration apprentice. She mainly works remotely, training learners and holding progress review meetings online. She regular uses Microsoft Forms to create tests to check her apprentices are developing and retaining the key knowledge they need.

Failure is not a permanent condition

With assessment comes outcomes and inevitably, apprentices will need to deal with making mistakes and experiencing failures as a key (and useful) part of their learning journey. Failure and mistakes are also often wrapped up with emotion and previous negative learning experiences for many apprentices.

A key part of the trainer's role is to help apprentices frame the outcomes of assessment, positive or negative, as data, rather than as a reflection of who they are. Making mistakes when learning new things is not the problem; it's what learners do next that matters. Failing helps us to learn; apprentices, tutors, coaches and employers can use the assessment data to inform subsequent actions and next steps as part of the training programme and work experience.

Employers may need to make adaptations at work, to give their apprentices more time to practise and consolidate their skills further, or to apply them in a different context or area of work. Off-the-job training sessions may need to be adapted by trainers, to revise and recap learning material where apprentices are not yet secure and require more expert instruction. The apprentice may need to use the outcomes of formative assessment to understand what they need to do to improve further, for example dedicating more time to responding to feedback, carrying out research or practising practical skills. Where apprentices make mistakes, these should largely be welcomed as a natural part of the learning process where apprentices are grappling with new content, concepts, processes and equipment.

It may be helpful to explore and discuss with apprentices how they feel about making mistakes, how they are likely to respond if they don't get something correct the first time, if they can't master a skill as fast as someone else. The mnemonics FAIL, SAIL and NAIL might be a useful reminder for apprentices tackling some challenging learning for the first time, to encourage persistence over time:

(1) **FAIL** = First Attempt In Learning

(2) **SAIL** = Second Attempt In Learning

(3) **NAIL** = Next Attempt In Learning

Whilst making mistakes can be a useful indicator that we are being challenged as we tackle something new and more complex, not all mistakes might be so helpful. Writer and speaker Eduardo Briceño (2015) suggests exploring different types of mistakes with our learners might be helpful to reduce the amount of unnecessary mistakes that they are making (Table 4.6).

REFLECTION POINT

- How do your apprentices feel when they make a mistake or fail at a particular task or activity?
- Would it be helpful to explore different types of mistake that learners make and how they should plan to deal and respond to these?
- What else could you do to help apprentices understand that failure is not a permanent condition and it's what they do next that counts?

In the next chapter, we will explore how apprentice's beliefs in their own abilities and skills can have an impact on their motivation and academic resilience, and how we can support them through regular progress reviews, tutorials and activities.

Table 4.6 Types of mistakes

Ah-ha moment mistakes	Stretch mistakes
This type of mistake may happen when we complete a task or action, and then realise in hindsight (upon gaining further information, data or insight) that this was a mistake. For example, an apprentice baker may have an ah-ha moment when their skills trainer highlights how they have overworked or underproved their dough, leading to a poor-quality product. This first-hand insight is useful, as the baker will know the next time and improve their bread baking technique.	Stretch mistakes are a good indication that we are working out of our comfort zone. They give us valuable information of what is going wrong, and how we might put it right to make progress. For example, an apprentice completing their Functional Skills maths practice tests might make a mistake as they work out a challenging calculation without support. Tutor feedback can help to identify the error and the action needed to improve, for example a worked example.
Sloppy mistakes	**High-stakes mistakes**
We've all made sloppy or silly mistakes in the past, when we should know better. These types of mistakes are when we do know how to do something but we're rushing, cutting corners or lacking in focus. We want to try and minimise these mistakes. For example, a customer service apprentice might be replying to a customer quickly by social media but makes various punctuation errors. They do know how to use the apostrophe correctly, but a lack of attention caused an embarrassing mistake. Learners should be encouraged to form an action plan to avoid these going forward, such as always proof-reading before hitting the send button.	These are mistakes that can have big consequences and therefore should be avoided. High-stakes mistakes can be time consuming or even dangerous, and therefore learners need to be careful to check their work and processes, so they are not made. For example, an apprentice scaffolder needs to erect scaffolds on pavements in public spaces. If they install the spurs and rakers outside of the correct operating angles, this could be dangerous. Trainers and employers need to ensure that apprentices are well supervised as they develop their skills to avoid these types of mistakes.

(Adapted from an idea by Briceño E. (2015) Mindset Works (www.mindsetworks.com))

A summary of key points

In this chapter we have looked at a number of key themes:

- different types of assessment methods, questioning techniques and types of feedback

- the importance of encouraging learners to regularly retrieve learning from their long-term memory

- how educators and employers can avoid over-supporting learners too quickly, so they can grapple, practise and master their skills

- the use of EdTech tools in formative assessment

- how exploring different types of mistakes can be helpful in learning.

Key links

Retrieval Practice www.retrievalpractice.org	Cognitive scientist, educator and author Pooja K. Agarwal, PhD website on retrieval practice provides a wealth of free resources including useful retrieval grids, charts and templates.
Getting Started with AFT from Cambridge Assessment www.apprenticeships.today/AFL	A useful free resource on assessment for learning, including questioning and feedback.

━━ FURTHER READING ━━━━━━━━━━━━━━━

Agarwal, P. K. and Bain, P. M. (2019) *Powerful Teaching*. San Francisco, CA: Jossey-Bass.

Bjork, E. and Bjork, R. (2009) Making Things Hard on Yourself, But in a Good Way: Creating Desirable Difficulties to Enhance Learning. In M. A. Gernsbacher and J. Pomerantz (eds.), *Psychology and the Real World*. New York, NY: Worth Publishers. Available at: https://bjorklab.psych.ucla.edu/wp-content/uploads/sites/13/2016/04/EBjork_RBjork_2011.pdf

Black, P. and Wiliam, D. (1999) *Assessment for Learning: Beyond the Black Box*. Cambridge: University of Cambridge School of Education.

Bradbury, A. and Wynne, V. (2020) *The Apprentice's Guide to End Point Assessment*. Los Angeles, CA: Learning Matters.

Cristodoulou, D. (2016) *Making Good Progress?: The Future of Assessment for Learning*. Oxford: Oxford University Press.

Csikszentmihalyi, M. (1990) *Flow: The Psychology of Optimal Experience*. New York, NY: Harper Perennial.

Hattie, J. (2012) *Visible Learning for Teachers, Maximising Impact on Learning*. Oxford: Routledge.

Jones, K. (2019) *Retrieval Practice*. Woodbridge: John Catt Educational.

Lemov, D. (2015) *Teach Like a Champion 2.0*. San Francisco, CA: Jossey-Bass.

Nottingham, J. (2016) *Challenging Learning*. Oxford: Routledge.

Nuthall, G. (2007) *The Hidden Lives of Learners*. Wellington: NZCER Press.

5
PROGRESS MONITORING, PERSONAL DEVELOPMENT AND TARGET SETTING

Hard work beats talent when talent doesn't work hard.

Tim Notke

— IN THIS CHAPTER —

In this chapter you will learn about:

- the importance of regular reviews of progress with all apprenticeship stakeholders
- how to develop the holistic learner including their academic resilience, metacognition and self-belief
- prioritising progress over processes or paperwork
- learner-centred coaching and mentoring techniques and action planning

This chapter has the following links to the assessor-coach apprenticeship standard (level 4):

Skills: the Assessor-Coach will be able to:	Knowledge: the Assessor-Coach will understand:
S2 apply or reference relevant initial and diagnostic assessment	K2 relevant forms of assessment to identify individual needs
S4 liaise with employers, colleagues and others to support learners' development	K4 additional support for learners available through workplace and provider-based colleagues

(Continued)

(Continued)

Skills: the Assessor-Coach will be able to:	Knowledge: the Assessor-Coach will understand:
S5 anticipate and overcome barriers to progress and inspire achievement, ensuring that learning is inclusive and supports diversity	K5 strategies for inspiring learners, increasing their resilience in overcoming barriers and obstacles, and in raising concerns
S7 give timely feedback on progress towards mastery of relevant skills and knowledge	K7 effective practice in giving feedback to guide progress and achievement
S11 use effective listening, assertiveness and questioning to support learners' to engage with their learning plans and with assessment criteria and processes	K11 the effective use of active listening, assertiveness and questioning skills to support retention, progress and achievement

Introduction

As we explored in Chapter 1, apprenticeships must last for a minimum of 12 months, to ensure that apprentices are developing substantial new knowledge, skills and behaviours. Many apprenticeships last significantly longer, especially for higher and degree level programmes. Over that time, learners may experience a range of different barriers to their learning including personal issues, time management challenges, changes at work, changes in trainers or training provider, redundancy, lack of confidence or motivation, failure of Functional Skills tests or the end-point assessment (EPA). The role of the assessor coach, or training consultant, is therefore key in ensuring that learners feel well supported and any barriers to their learning can be overcome.

Support will include regular formal reviews of progress, involving tripartite meetings with the employer representative, assessor coach and apprentice. The setting of clear and challenging targets and actions plans will also help to motivate learners to keep them moving forward in the development of knowledge and skills. Pastoral support and support for additional learning needs may also be provided where required. The coach may provide signposting and referrals to other colleagues, departments and external agencies that can help the apprentice to overcome any barriers to their learning.

The assessor coach may be providing the vocational skills training as well as taking on the role of monitoring and supporting the apprentices' learning journey. Alternatively, the learner may have a range of professionals supporting their progress, for example the vocational trainer, learning mentor, Functional Skills tutor and skills coach. Where this is the case, the assessor coach needs to liaise regularly with all stakeholders, to ensure that the full, holistic picture of progress is captured. This information can be used to make judgements on the rate and level of progress the apprentice is making, in line with the individual learning plan.

The employer has a key part to play in this formal review process, as they can make judgements on the impact of the on- and off-the-job training on the apprentice's role and how they carry out their duties at work. The employer representative at the progress review meeting may present a summary of feedback from the apprentice's colleagues or supervisor, for example. The apprentice should also take a proactive role in the review of their progress, taking into account feedback from customers or clients and their own self-assessment of their progress so far, using evidence where possible to make judgements as accurate as possible. Figure 5.1 highlights all the different stakeholders and forms of evidence that could be used in a formal progress review.

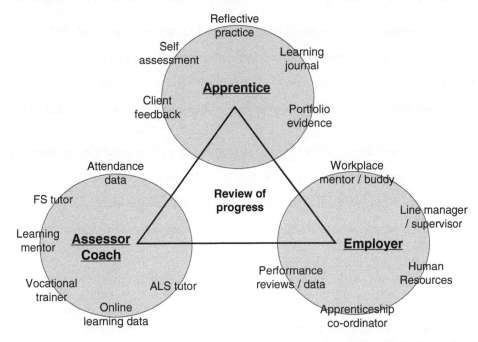

Figure 5.1 Apprentice progress review stakeholders and evidence

Together as a partnership, the employer, coach and apprentice can review the progress made from the learner's starting points, and identify where additional challenge, support, assessments or work experience are required to keep them moving forward towards achieving occupational competency, going through the gateway and then formal accreditation following EPA. These formal reviews may identify that adaptations are required to the apprentice's plan of training and learning. For example, they may need some additional time away from their normal work role to focus on training and skills development. The apprentice may need to take a formal break in their learning, for example due to ill health, pregnancy or to care for a family member. The learner needs to expand their role or duties at work in order to gain confidence and experience across all areas of the apprenticeship standard.

A measure of progress

In Chapter 2, we explored the importance of the initial assessment and induction process at identifying apprentice's starting points. A key part of the formal review process is to make a judgement on the progress that apprentices are making, if they are developing substantial and significant new skills, knowledge and behaviours, and if they are being well prepared for their summative assessments and progressing to their next steps. Assessor, coaches and training consultants therefore need a secure understanding of what 'progress' is. As we explored in Chapter 3, progress is not necessarily the completion of modules, units, formative assessments and paperwork; it is the vocational knowledge, practical and technical skills, and professional workplace behaviours that apprentices are learning, developing, applying and mastering. It may be useful to consider some of the following questions:

- does the apprentice know more about their role, their industry and their employer?

- are they able to carry out more tasks, functions and processes safely and professionally at work?

- are they able to work with more accuracy, independence and confidence?

- do they understand the reasons behind what they are doing and can they ask for help and support when they need to?

- are they able to effectively apply what they are learning in different situations and contexts?

- what more do they know and can do now than at the last review?

- where does the apprentice need to improve further and what are the main priorities?

- what additional support do they need in order to stay on track and make progress in line with high expectations?

Formal reviews may return to the initial assessments carried out at the start of the learning programme in order to try and quantify the progress made in each of the knowledge, skills and behaviours that make up the standard. Coaches and employers should guide these judgements with the apprentice, so they are based on evidence and examples, rather than just a 'feeling' of progress.

Many training providers make use of sophisticated software to make judgements on progress over time. However, many of these programmes often base the progress measure on the completion of assignments and observations. It could be that an apprentice has made significant process in areas of their learning that are a priority for them, for example in their communication skills, level of independence and confidence, in their theoretical understanding or ability to apply their practical skills. However, unless a formal assessment has been completed, marked, tracked and mapped to specific standards or criteria, this 'progress' may not be formally recognised. Conversely, a more experienced apprentice may have completed a raft of assessment checkpoints and milestones which were all straightforward and required little or no development of *new* knowledge or skills. Therefore, the software may highlight significant rates of progression when in fact the individual learner may not have developed any substantial new knowledge or skills.

CASE STUDY

Paul is a skills coach working with Jade, an apprentice completing her operations and departmental manager apprenticeship at level 5. Paul has only recently taken over supporting Jade as part of his caseload of apprentices, as her previous coach left the organisation to take up a promotion with an alternative provider. Luckily, the previous coach has completed the initial assessment skills scan which has been updated at Jade's last two progress reviews, where her area manager was also present. Below is an extract from the review paperwork which explores one of the key skills areas of communication which is part of Jade's apprenticeship standard:

Skill 7 Communication:	Emerging (just starting)	Developing (showing an increased competence)	Secure (meeting competence expectations most of the time)	Mastered (demonstrating full competence consistently)
S7.2 Able to chair meetings and present using a range of media	✔ (IA) ✔ (PR1)	✔ (PR2)		
S7.3 Use of active listening, and able to challenge and give constructive feedback		✔ (IA)	✔ (PR1)	✔ (PR2)

Evidence/rationale for judgement

Initial assessment: Jade has worked for the local authority library service for the last 15 years and has moved from a lending assistant, to team leader, and is now in a new role as the library manager. She has carried out some informal presentations in the past but has never chaired meetings or used a range of different communication media, but this will be a key expectation of this new role. Jade has some experience of active listening and has had to give constructive feedback to staff in her team leading role.

Progress review 1: Jade you have focused on developing your practical communication skills in preparation for carrying out appraisals of your team. You have completed an online module on active listening, and this has developed your understanding of how to make colleagues feel valued and listened to as part of the performance review process. You have worked with your area manager to gain a secure understanding of the appraisal process and the paperwork required. You have not yet started to prepare for chairing your first meeting as the library manager, but this is approaching and will be a key focus on your learning over the next quarter.

Progress review 2: Jade you have demonstrated strong progress in developing and applying your skills in giving effective challenging and constructive feedback to your colleagues, verbally and in writing, through the performance review process. You have practised and mastered your active listening skills to ensure colleagues feel valued but key objectives for improvement are set. You have completed your first formal meeting as Chair, setting the agenda, leading discussions and ensuring all participants had a voice. You will be working on your multimedia skills over the next three months, in order to Chair your next meeting using Microsoft Teams, sharing your screen and using a PPT presentation. Your manager has invited you to shadow a regional meeting to see these techniques in action.

Looking at the detailed notes, Paul is able to track Jade's progress and has a good idea of what her development priorities are. He now needs to arrange the third review and set some appropriately challenging targets in line with her learning plan. Jade's next review is well overdue given the change in coach. She is keen to carry out the review as soon as possible but her area manager is away on leave for the next three weeks.

(Continued)

(Continued)

REFLECTIVE QUESTIONS

- What are the advantages and disadvantages of the review notes that Jade's previous assessor coach has completed?

- Would you set up the next review even through Jade's manager is not available? What alternatives are available?

- How would explore what progress Jade has made since her last review and what actions and targets might you be setting to ensure she is on track to complete?

Engaging the employer

The role of the employer representative in formal reviews is essential. They are best placed to make judgements of the application of the apprentices' knowledge, skills and behaviours in the workplace, and the positive impact they are having on the organisation. The employer will see first-hand the impact the on- and off-the-job training has had and how this is translated into the duties carried out by the apprentice. The employer can also update the skills coach on any developments at work, or highlight any helpful projects or additional responsibilities that the apprentice can take on to extend and further develop their applied skills and behaviours.

Employers are busy, and it can be difficult to secure their attendance at reviews. Where this is not possible, their input should be captured and acknowledged in other ways, for example a pre-meeting with the coach at a convenient time, or a written summary of the apprentice's progress and areas requiring further development. An alternative workplace representative may be able to contribute on the line manager's behalf, for example a training manager or apprenticeship co-ordinator, to ensure the tripartite nature of the process is maintained.

As we explored in earlier chapters, apprentices must be well supported by their employers to access at least their minimum off-the-job training entitlement. Staffing issues, seasonality and staff turnover can all have an impact on the ability of employers to release apprentices for the required learning time, as agreed when completing the apprenticeship commitment at the start of the training programme. Whilst it can be challenging for employers to deal with unforeseen circumstances, apprentices must receive the learning and training entitlement, whether that's as a day release to attend training at a local provider, as a block placement, time to carry out high-quality online learning or protected time to meet with trainers, coaches and assessors on the employer premises.

A key part of the review process will be to review the ongoing accrual of off-the-job training hours to ensure the apprentice is benefitting from their minimum entitlement. Where this is not happening, skills coaches must act swiftly to work with the employer to resolve the issues quickly, reminding them of their commitment, so that learning time is not lost and the apprentices make very slow progress. The review should focus on the *impact* of the training, rather than just a check of hours completed.

Progress not process

Most training providers will use specific paperwork, or online systems, to document the review process. Whilst this is important to capture the discussions, reflections, judgements and actions, the review of progress should not be process-led, driven by the completion of tick boxes and audit documentation. As we explored in the last chapter, the key focus needs to be on developing a secure and shared understanding of where the apprentice is now, relative to where they started, and what they need to do in order to close the gap to get to where they need to be. This learning journey is likely to be a very unique and personalised one for each apprentice. Each learner with have their own spikey profile of existing skills and competencies, as well as priorities for development. They will make progress at different speeds and at different times. Each may encounter different barriers to their learning which will need to be overcome.

Much like the air traffic controller who needs to carefully monitor all the different positions, warning signs, weather indicators and data readings for the different aircraft they are controlling, the skills coach too needs to take constant readings for their caseload of apprentices, to ensure they are developing holistically and making substantial progress towards their destination. For example:

- development of technical knowledge, practical skills and vocational behaviours

- attendance and punctuality at training sessions and at work

- personal, social, welfare and safeguarding issues

- effectiveness of support for any additional learning needs or disabilities

- applied English, maths and ICT skills, study and research skills

- initiative, communication, team working and employability skills

- self-awareness, independence, confidence, motivation and attitude

- understanding of how to be a good citizen and member of an inclusive and tolerant society

- timely achievement of specific targets and actions.

The coach may need to take action to ensure the apprentice is still on route to their destination, and is able to weather any storms that may be part of the journey. As we can see from the list of possible progress indicators, the review should focus on much more than just the achievement of unit or module assessments. Rather than a tick box exercise which records the completion of tasks, the review process should explore the holistic development of the apprentice, and the inter-relation and co-dependency of their personal, academic and vocational development. A learner who is struggling with personal and welfare issues is unlikely to be able to maximise their academic and skills development. An apprentice who is struggling to manage their time, meet their targets or turn up at training sessions may be at risk of not completing their apprenticeship or securing full-time employment in the future. A learner who lacks academic resilience may not be able to respond positively to constructive feedback and challenging targets.

Apprentices' role in a modern, tolerant and inclusive society

A key aspect of the apprenticeship training programme is also to develop apprentices' understanding of how to be an effective member of a modern, tolerant and inclusive society, challenging any stereotypes and prejudices they may hold and developing their meaningful understanding of equality and diversity. The review process offers a useful opportunity to explore these values and how they are being developed and reinforced throughout all aspects of the training and work experience, including on- and off-the-job training, and support from managers, supervisors and mentors.

The review process should avoid tokenistic completion of tick boxes and check points and instead probe apprentice's understanding of key issues that affect their role in the organisation, as well as the wider society, for example.

- Do apprentices understand the possible risks to their health, safety and wellbeing inside and outside of work and how to assess and minimise these risks?

- Are apprentices developing a deep understanding of the role and the responsibilities they have both as a member of an organisation and of a modern, tolerant and inclusive society?

- What further support and guidance do apprentices need to help them uphold and contribute to the principles of democracy, the rule of law, individual liberty and mutual respect, in their day-to-day work roles and outside the working environment?

- How do apprentices help to create, support and promote an inclusive environment that celebrates difference and diversity at work, in the office, on the pitch, on the building site or in the salon?

It will be useful to spend some time to explore specific examples with learners and to identify ways to further support and deepen their understanding of these key values and beliefs, so they can be ambassadors for their organisations, as well as contributing to a civil, fair and accepting society.

Pastoral support

Apprentices may be school leavers with little or no prior experience of the workplace. They may be experienced colleagues who have many years' experience in the role but have not completed any formal learning for many years. Apprentices may be dealing with challenging personal circumstances, such as:

- physical or mental health problems

- housing, budgeting and financial issues

- relationship and emotional difficulties

- addiction and substance misuse

- workplace performance issues, capability, grievance or disciplinary matters

- time management, self-care and motivational challenges.

It may be appropriate for the skills coach to try and support some of these issues, or encourage apprentices to speak with their employers and access their support mechanisms. It may also be necessary to signpost or refer apprentices to appropriate external agencies who can offer more specialist advice, guidance and support, for example counselling or health services. There may be occasions where apprentices are dealing with issues which may impact on their health, safety and wellbeing. Training providers will have specific safeguarding policies and procedures in place, where trainers, coaches and learners themselves can make referrals to dedicated safeguarding officers to make the necessary risk assessments and provide specific support where required.

Academic resilience

As well as pastoral issues, the review process may identify apprentices who lack confidence, self-belief and resilience in their learning. Academic resilience is characterised by learners' ability to:

- use skills to cope and recover from problems and challenges

- adapt well in the face of adversity and threats

- bounce back from difficult experiences and critical feedback

- deal positively with disappointment and failure.

In a learning situation, Martin and Marsh (2008) also describe the notion of 'academic buoyancy' as the ability of learners to successfully deal with academic setbacks and challenges that are typical of a learning programme or course of study. Some of the typical challenges that apprentices may face in their learning programme could be:

- when their training or job role becomes more difficult or complex

- when feedback from trainers or managers is critical and constructive

- when they have experienced failure or don't know the answer

- when they are under the pressure of multiple deadlines

- when the outcomes of assignments, tests and assessments are poor.

Low levels of academic resilience or buoyancy may be influenced by apprentice's previous academic experiences at school. They may have a history of low achievement or failing exams. Learners may believe they are not 'naturally' clever or smart, and have low levels of self-efficacy, the belief in how likely they are to be successful in a particular task or subject area. Where learners hold the belief that their abilities are fixed, learners may well feel that additional, more challenging learning is beyond their capabilities, with a risk that they may drop out and quit their apprenticeship. This may present as a lack of engagement, absence or even disruptive behaviour.

This view of 'intelligence' as an entity fixed at birth through genetics, rather than as something which can be nurtured and incrementally developed, can lead to low levels of self-belief, self-efficacy and self-esteem. Over the last four decades, the research of Professor Carol Dweck (2012) has provided persuasive evidence that learners who hold a 'growth mindsets' belief more of the time (a belief that abilities are fluid and changeable over time), may respond more profitably and proactively to challenges and setbacks in their learning, than those who hold more of a fixed mindset belief (a belief that abilities are fixed and unlikely to change).

Learners with a predominantly growth mindset belief are more likely to seek out challenges, show greater persistence and resilience in the face of difficulties and be more open to learning from their mistakes and the feedback from their trainers and coach. Learners with a more fixed mindset belief have a view that although you can learn new things, you can't really change how intelligent or able you are. Learners with a more fixed mindset belief might have very set beliefs about particular subjects, topics and tasks they are just 'no good at', for example maths, or drawing or presenting to other people. Table 5.1 explores some of the key differences, and consequences in learning, of holding a predominantly fixed and growth belief about ability and intelligence.

Table 5.1 Growth versus fixed mindset summary

Mindset:	Fixed belief	Growth belief
Your belief:	Intelligence is a fixed trait	Intelligence is cultivated through learning
Your priority:	'Look smart', not thick	Become smarter, through learning
You feel smart, when:	Achieving easy, low effort successes and when outperforming others	Engaging fully with new tasks, exerting effort, stretching and applying skills
You avoid:	Effort, difficulty, setbacks, higher-performing peers	Easy, previously mastered tasks – *boring and no progress*
Challenges and trials:	Avoid them – *they will lead to failure and embarrassment*	Embrace them – *failing provides data to help us learn better*
Feedback and criticism:	Ignore, even if useful – what's the point if I can't profit from it?	Use it and learn from it – the steps to help me succeed
Effort and persistence:	Fruitless – *why bother if you haven't got the ability to do better?*	The path to mastery – *purposeful practice make progress*
Community and collaboration:	Threatened by success of others – *their success highlights my lack of success*	Inspired by it – *what can I learn from others about how they do it?*

(Adapted from Hymer, 2009)

Nurturing a 'growth mindset'

To try and harness the benefits of the growth mindset belief, it may be necessary for trainers, coaches and employers to spend some time helping apprentices to challenge their fixed mindset responses and reactions at time when they feel challenged or when they have experienced failure. Exploring how our brain works, how it responds to learning and challenges, how it develops and strengthens new neural connections even in later adult life, has been found in some studies to be helpful in encouraging learners to persist when they first encounter challenges and don't find immediate success.

── TAKE IT FURTHER ──

Studies of London cab drivers by scientists at University College London found that when they had completed studying for 'The Knowledge', a huge two to four year special memory test of 320 routes, covering 25,000 streets and 20,000 landmarks and places of interest, the size of their hippocampus, part of the brain that deals with learning and memory, had grown. This helps to illustrate the plasticity of the human brain, and how it can physically grow and develop new cells through learning in adult life. When apprentices struggle to master new learning straightaway, this is a useful example to highlight the need for persistence, as they are not there 'yet'.

As we explored in the last chapter, focussing our feedback on the learning process, rather than on the person, will also be helpful in recognising and reinforcing positive and useful learning strategies and approaches. Although it may not feel intuitively right, Professor Dweck offers a useful reminder to educators to avoid the lure of giving praise to learners for quick wins and completion of easy tasks:

> It has become common practice to praise students for their performance on easy tasks, to tell them they are smart when they do something quickly and perfectly. When we do this, we are not teaching them to welcome challenge and learn from errors. We are teaching them that easy success means they are intelligent and, by implication, that errors and effort mean they are not.

> *(Dweck, 2012, p. 43)*

So although it can be tempting to lavish apprentices with lots of person-centred praise when they have completed tasks and activities which are easily achievable and straightforward, it is likely to be more beneficial for learning in the long term, to raise their expectations to engage with more challenging learning. In this way, we can begin to reinforce that a meaningful success requires effort. When apprentices have made significant progress in their learning journey, it is helpful to provide feedback on these areas specifically, for example:

- *I can see how you have really focussed on developing your accuracy and attention to detail in your written reports. The layout, presentation and use of paragraphs are now much improved compared with your earlier submissions – very well done.*

- *I know how much of a challenge it is for you presenting to other people. You have really stepped up to this challenge and your verbal communication skills have improved significantly. You can speak with confidence and get your point across fluently – great work.*

- *Looking at your reference lists, I can see how you are now using a much broader range of valid and reliable information sources to support your arguments. Your Harvard referencing skills are also much more accurate now – fantastic progress.*

- *Your precision and accuracy with your knife skills have improved greatly over the last 12 weeks. You can now work much more quickly, efficiently and safely in the kitchen and I know your manager is impressed – good job.*

Investing in 'learning to learn'

Do your apprentices know what 'effort' is? Do they know what to do, when they don't know what to do? Are they able to work independently and direct their own learning when you are not there? Do they rely on you to spoon-feed every task, target and activity for them? One of the criticisms of employers with the older style of apprenticeships was that apprentices could achieve a range of qualifications but not have the self-awareness, initiative and confidence required to carry out their roles and meet the needs of the workplace.

As we have explored, a key part of any new apprenticeship is to develop learners into independent and effective members of the workplace, who can consistently meet occupational standards. The role of trainers, coaches and mentors therefore is to develop the whole apprentice, including their confidence, initiative, resourcefulness, study skills and resilience to deal with things that don't always go according to plan. If an apprentice is too reliant on the support and direction of their mentors and tutors, then you may find they struggle to study independently between training sessions. They may not be able to deal with problems and setbacks when completing their projects, assessments or research. They may lack the confidence and initiative to know what to do when they come across a new situation or challenge at work. When they hit a challenge point, they may lose confidence and motivation and their progress may stall.

Using strategies, resources and tools to developing apprentices' metacognitive skills will help them to become more self-aware, as they learn not just about the subject knowledge or technical skills needed for a specific task, but also more about the way they learn, think and react. Developing this level of self-awareness will help apprentices to grow as lifelong learners and to take more responsibility for their own learning. Time spent on developing learners' metacognitive skills will help them to become more confident in how to react and respond to different situations, to use their initiative when faced with unforeseen events, to take alterative courses of action when needed and to reflect on and evaluate themselves and their actions.

Figure 5.2 highlights different levels of metacognition, from learners who turn up at work and training sessions waiting to be told what to do and when to do it, to strategic and reflective learners who are able to direct their own learning, choose the resources that support their learning best and identify when they need more challenge, or more support.

To encourage this shift to a more self-aware, reflective approach to learning, trainers and coaches can explicitly encourage apprentices to follow different metacognitive stages or a cycle which focuses on the learning process. Apprentices should regularly be encouraged to *plan* how they will approach learning something new, for example taking on a new project at work which allows them to apply

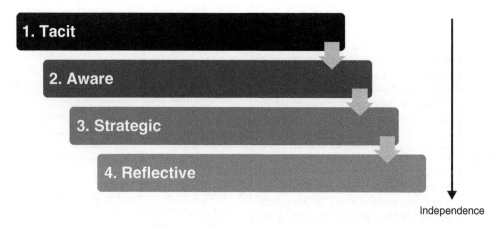

Figure 5.2 Developing student's metacognition (adapted from Perkins, 1992)

what they have learnt in the classroom. They should know how to *monitor* how their plan is going, to identify if they need to make any changes and how to go about this. Apprentices should *evaluate* how effective their learning plan and actions were, for example their approach, the processes they followed, and the resources they used. They should identify how they could use what they have learnt, for example on new projects, in different situations or with different clients.

Following this systematic metacognitive process can help apprentices to become more self-aware of how they learn and when they need to take responsibility for making changes. Figure 5.3 shows the three main stages of the metacognitive cycle.

This deliberate process of planning their approach to a given learning task, activity or experience can be quite difficult for apprentices at first. To assist them in this process, it may be helpful to ask a series of different questions at each stage, which encourages them to focus on the *process* of learning (Table 5.2).

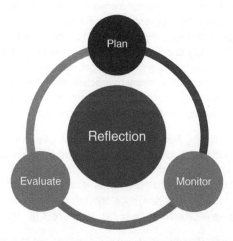

Figure 5.3 Stages of the metacognitive cycle (adapted from https://cambridge-community.org.uk/professional-development/gswmeta/index.html)

Table 5.2 Metacognitive questioning

Plan	Apprentices should think about the learning goal their trainer or manager has set, and consider how they will approach the task and which strategies they could use to meet the objective.	• What am I being asked to do? • Which strategies will I use? • Are there any strategies that I have used before that might be useful? • What might be a barrier to success? • Will I need any support and from who?
Check	Apprentices implement their plan and monitor the progress they are making towards their learning goal. They might decide to make changes to the strategies they are using if these are not working.	• Is the strategy that I am using working? • Do I need to try something different? • What information have I got that can help me to understand if I am moving in the right direction? • Should I ask for advice and guidance?
Review	Apprentices should determine how successful the plan and strategies they have used were in helping them to achieve their learning goal. They can then use this insight on future tasks, jobs and projects. They may use feedback from others.	• How well did I do? • What didn't go well? • What could I do differently next time? • What other types of problem can I use this strategy for? • Have I learnt anything new about myself?

CASE STUDY

Katie works for a special needs charity in the business development department. She is one year into completing her level 5 operations/departmental manager apprenticeship. She attends a face-to-face classroom training session with other apprentices once a month, as well as online webinars every two weeks. Katie has access to online, self-paced learning modules which she can complete at any time. Katie is supported by her skills coach Ade, who visits her in the workplace every eight weeks to carry out observations, performance reviews and to meet with her manager to discuss projects and tasks she could take on to help her apply theory to practice. Out of work, Katie is a volunteer leader for her local Girlguiding unit. She enjoys organising activities and fundraising events, leading a team of helpers, and making sure health, safety and safeguarding policies are followed.

Katie is enjoying her apprenticeship but is finding learning at level 5 a challenge. She often emails her tutors and coach for additional advice and support and to check she is 'doing it right'. Her tutors set her research tasks but she finds the amount of information available online overwhelming and often fails to find what she needs. Ade has noticed that Katie struggles with her written work. She doesn't always reference the information sources she has used in her assignments, or use paragraphs effectively to break up her text for the reader.

Katie's attendance at training sessions and reviews is excellent but she often doesn't complete the learning activities she is set between sessions. Her manager is becoming concerned that she is making slow progress and is not developing the confidence and skills she needs as part of her business development role, such as writing bids, managing contracts and generating income in line with the business strategy.

REFLECTIVE QUESTIONS

- Katie is engaged but lacks the confidence and study skills she needs. How could Ade use the metacognitive cycle to help her improve?
- How could Katie use the process of 'plan – monitor – evaluate' to develop her self-awareness and transferable skills between her management roles at work and when volunteering?
- How could Katie's manager, Ade, and her vocational tutors, all work together to set a workplace project that Katie could use to develop her study skills, independence and confidence?

Katie is clearly motivated, organised and has a lot of useful skills she has developed in her volunteering role. It may be helpful to encourage Katie to specifically plan how she will approach her next work-place learning project, rather than over-relying on her tutors, or avoiding the task when she is not clear on what to do. For example:

- Katie could have a meeting with Ade, and her manager, to negotiate an appropriate project that she could take on at work to develop her skills and independence. She can ask for specific targets and outcomes that will help her to monitor her progress

- she could ask Ade for guidance on a few specific sources of valid and reliable information that would support her research and keep her focused

- she could complete an online learning module on referencing different information sources

- she could ask her peers for guidance on how to use paragraphs effectively and to see examples of their work as a guide

- she could schedule a brief weekly meeting with her manager to review her progress on the project to keep her on track

- she could send a draft copy of her written work to Ade for formative assessment and feedback two weeks before the deadline, so she has time to make any changes.

It is important that Katie's tutors and coaches challenge her to develop her self-awareness as a learner, to ensure she develops the independence and autonomy she will need to thrive in her role and to achieve her apprenticeship. Learning strategies and approaches which may have worked well for her at school may no longer be as effective for her on her apprenticeship, where she is required to demonstrate applied skills and behaviours required in her workplace role.

Coaching and mentoring for success

As we have explored with Katie above, it may be necessary to encourage and support apprentices to take more responsibilities for their learning, rather than becoming dependent on their assessor, tutor or trainer. The terms coaching and mentoring are sometimes used interchangeably, and there are clear crossovers in their main purpose and objective to help the apprentice develop, grow and achieve. There are some generally accepted distinctions, with coaching often viewed as a more short-term but formal relationship, focused on encouraging the coachee to reflect on their own progress, set new goals and targets and identify steps and actions to achieve these. Sometimes mentoring is seen as a longer-term relationship with an experienced colleague who has significant vocational experience in a particular field, role or subject area. It is common for apprentices to work with a workplace mentor or buddy, to learn from a more experience colleague and role model.

Mentors should be role models for their apprentices, demonstrating high standards of vocational expertise and upholding and exemplifying professional standards. They should showcase how the role is to be carried out, using their expertise and experience to model how to complete jobs and tasks efficiently and effectively, safely and competently. As we explored in the last chapter, mentors may need to correct at times, but often could use modelling, cueing and prompting to guide the apprentice as they develop their confidence, independence and skills. Mentors should develop their questioning and listening skills to challenge and support apprentices when appropriate, encouraging them to explain their choices, and how they could improve their skills further, before offering their advice, guidance and experience.

Alred et al (1998) identify a number of useful mentoring methods to help apprentices explore their progress and develop their skills and competencies:

- ask open and close questions

- listen and challenge

- recognise strengths and weaknesses

- establish priorities

- give information and advice

- share experiences and tell stories.

A range of useful models can help to guide coaching and mentoring conversations during review meetings such as GROW, LEAP or FUEL. Sir John Whitmore (2009) is credited with developing the popular 'GROW' coaching model which aims to unlock potential following a cycle that explores an individuals' goals, the reality of the situation, possible opportunities and their will to commit to taking action. The following table explores some questions which could be asked by the coach at each stage in the process (Table 5.3).

Table 5.3 GROW model

Goal	• What do you want to achieve?
	• What would achieving this lead to in the long term?
	• When would you like to achieve this by?
Reality	• What is your current position?
	• What stops you from moving on?
Options	• What could you do?
	• What else?
	• And what else?
Will	• What will you do?
	• What will be the first step?

(Based on Whitmore, 2009)

Tolhurst (2010) proposes the LEAP model as useful but similar alternative framework (Table 5.4).

Table 5.4 LEAP model

L	E	A	P
Looking at goals	Exploring reality	Analysing possibilities	Planning action

(Based on Tolhurst, 2010)

In their book *The Extraordinary Coach: How the Best Leaders Help Others Grow*, John Zenger and Kathleen Stinnett outline their 'FUEL' framework for managing coaching conversations and encouraging coaches to fully explore the current situation before exploring possibilities and practical ways forward (Table 5.5).

A coaching approach can be a supportive and useful way to encourage apprentices to fully understand their current situation, overcome barriers to their learning and progress and feel more in control of taking actions to improve a given situation for them, rather than the assessor or trainer imposing a series of actions on the learner, that they may feel no ownership of.

— TAKE IT FURTHER —

Developed by Professor Gabriel Oettingen (2015) as a result of over 20 years of scientific research, 'WOOP', also known as Mental Contrasting with Implementation Intentions (MCII), is an evidence-based strategy that can be used to change behaviour and overcome barriers to development, growth and progress. WOOP standards for Wish, Outcome, Obstacle and Plan. Supported by tutors or coaches, apprentices can be encourage to complete an exercise to help them identify specific actions to overcome obstacles in their learning or in their personal or professional lives.

- What is your most important academic **wish** or concern?
- What would be the best thing, the best **outcome** about fulfilling your Wish?

(Continued)

(Continued)

- What is your main **obstacle** that stands in the way of you fulfilling your Wish? What is it within you that holds you back from fulfilling your Wish?

- What can you do to overcome your obstacle? Name one effective action you can take. When and where will the obstacle occur the next time?

- Make the following **plan:** *If...* (Obstacle), *Then* I will ...(action)

For example, an apprentice struggling to stay focused on their test revision may follow the following plan:

> **IF** *I am finding it difficult to focus on my EPA practice tests because I get distracted by my mobile phone and social media,* **THEN** *I will download and use a free app which restricts notifications and distractions, such as Forest or SPACE.*

Find out more about this helpful, evidence-based strategy at: www.woopmylife.org

Table 5.5 FUEL framework

Frame the conversation	Use questions which allows the coach and apprentice to agree on the purpose, process and outcome of the coaching conversation.	• What would you like to discuss? • Why is this important to you? • What would you like to achieve from this process?
Understand the current state	It is important to explore how the apprentice views the current situation, how they feel, what alternatives there could be and what the sticking points are.	• Can you tell we what's happening? • How does that make you feel? • Is there any other reason this could be the case? • What is working well? • What do you feel needs to change?
Explore the desired state	Explore what a successful outcome would look like, the possibilities available and the different ways to get there.	• What would a successful outcome be for you? • What are the possibilities? • How can we move forward with this situation?
Lay out a success plan	Now it is time to identify the specific actions and next steps that will move the apprentice towards their desired state.	• What is the first step? • What are the key milestones? • When will this be completed by? • What assistance do you need?

(Adapted from Zenger and Stinnett, 2010)

FIND OUT MORE

Why not explore coaching skills in more detail by taking an online course. OpenLearn, from the Open University, provides a free online course exploring explore ideas about coaching and mentoring, along with practical guidance and examples to follow.

Find out more at: www.apprenticeships.today/coaching

Target setting

As we have explored with the different models of coaching, the use of specific target setting is a key part of committing the apprentice to taking effective action towards a desired future. When carrying out progress reviews, assessors, coaches, mentors and employers should consider the holistic development of the apprentices including their subject specific knowledge and skills, their learning and study skills, their applied English and maths skills, as well as their pastoral needs and work commitments. The regular tripartite meeting is therefore so important to ensure all these needs and specific priorities are managed and recorded in a way that supports the apprentice's timely progress but in a way which is manageable, realistic and achievable.

The use of the SMART acronym is often used to guide the target setting process to add clarity and precision to goal setting:

- **S**pecific

- **M**easurable

- **A**chievable

- **R**ealistic

- **T**ime-bound

However, care should also be taken to ensure that targets are focused on the knowledge, skills and behaviours to be developed, rather than simply a list of tasks and activities. This focus on mastery goals and specific learning objectives will help apprentices to see the purpose and value in their action plans, rather than a collection of evidence requirements to meet audit or internal quality assurance purposes (Table 5.6).

Apprentices may respond well to SMART action plans that clearly identify and record their next steps. Learners must also feel some ownership of these targets and goals if they are to invest in their achievement, especially when they may be dealing with significant personal issues or are very busy in their work role. Try and provide clear signposts and specific links to learning resources that may support apprentices in completing their learning actions, rather than more vague references to accessing online materials that may help.

Table 5.6 *Better target setting*

Less effective targets	More effective targets
Please work on and submit the rest of Module 6 in the next four weeks.	Carry out research using the websites suggested, to develop your understanding of current safeguarding legislation and the impact on nurseries and pre-schools. Email your summary in the next 10 working days.
Complete two FS maths practice papers by the next review visit, achieving at least 70 per cent.	By the next review visit, complete the five past paper questions to consolidate your knowledge of how to calculate area, perimeter and volume accurately.
Take care with your spelling and grammar - please proofread all your formative assignment submissions.	Complete exercises 2B and 2C to further develop your understanding of the correct use of apostrophes, and upload within the next two weeks.
Improve your attendance and punctuality at training sessions - this needs to be above 80 per cent.	Book and attend a meeting with your Learning Mentor in the next two weeks, to develop your time management strategies and to discuss ways to catch up on training sessions missed.

A summary of key points

In this chapter we have looked at a number of key themes:

- how to involve all stakeholders in the regular reviews of apprentices' progress, and the setting of clear actions for development

- the importance of supporting the development of the whole apprentice, including their character, resilience, self-belief and key values

- the value of prioritising progress over completion of processes or paperwork

- how learner-centred approaches to coaching and mentoring can help apprentices to make progress towards their desired goals.

Key links

Chartered Institute of Personnel and Development (CIPD) www.apprenticeships.today/CIPD	The CIPD website provides a range of useful articles and resources on coaching and mentoring in the workplace.

Excellence Gateway from the Education and Training Foundation www.excellencegateway.org.uk	The Excellent Gateway has over 7,000 online resources to support trainers, tutors and coaches including materials using learner-centred motivational dialogue to achieve change.
Character Lab www.characterlab.org	Character Lab is a non-profit organisation that connects research and educational practice. The website includes free resources, advice and guidance on how to develop learner's character, including grit, growth mindset, self-control and emotional intelligence.

■■ FURTHER READING

Alred, G., Garvey, B. and Smith, R. (1998) *Mentoring Pocketbook*. Alresford: Management Pocketbooks.

Dweck, C. (2012) *Mindset: How You Can Fulfil Your Potential*. London: Robinson Publishing.

Hymer, B. (2009) *Gifted & Talented Pocketbook*. Alresford: Teachers' Pocketbooks.

Kehoe, D. (2007) *Practice Makes Perfect: The Importance of Practical Learning*. London: The Social Market Foundation.

Lockyer, S. (2015) *Thinking About Thinking*. London: Teacherly Publications.

Oettingen, G. (2015) *Rethinking Positive Thinking: Inside the New Science of Motivation*. New York, NY: Current.

Swainston, T. (2017) *A Mindset for Success*. Carmarthen, Wales: Crown House Publishing.

Tolhurst, J. (2010) *The Essential Guide to Coaching and Mentoring*, 2nd ed. London: Pearson Education Limited.

Whitmore, J. (2009) *Coaching for Performance: GROWing Human Potential and Purpose: The Principles and Practice of Coaching and Leadership, People Skills for Professionals*, 4th ed. London: Nicholas Brealey Publishing.

Zenger, J. and Stinnett, K. (2010) *The Extraordinary Coach: How the Best Leaders Help Others Grow*. New York, NY: McGraw-Hill Education.

6

MEETING THE REQUIREMENTS OF HIGH-QUALITY APPRENTICESHIPS

Every teacher needs to improve, not because they are not good enough, but because they can be even better.

Professor Dylan Wiliam

IN THIS CHAPTER

In this chapter you will learn about:

- the importance of quality assurance in delivering high-quality apprenticeships
- the impact of continuous professional development (CPD) on vocational and pedagogical skills
- the professional standards expected of those working with the new apprenticeships
- the importance of working and learning from other apprenticeship stakeholders

This chapter has the following links to the assessor-coach apprenticeship standard (level 4):

Skills: the Assessor-Coach will be able to:	Knowledge: the Assessor-Coach will understand:
S12 comply with awarding organisation requirements and local quality and safety guidelines	K12 the quality and safety requirements of assessment and procedures for reporting concerns

(Continued)

(Continued)

Skills: the Assessor-Coach will be able to:	Knowledge: the Assessor-Coach will understand:
S13 support peer review and quality assurance procedures	K13 internal and external quality procedures and the role of peer review
S15 maintain the currency of their own knowledge and skills, with reference to workplace practice and feedback from others	K15 how to maintain occupational currency and ways to improve coaching and professional practice

Introduction

Throughout each chapter, we have explored key ideas, approaches and tools for planning, delivering and assessing high-quality apprenticeships.

In chapter one, we explored the ethos and development of the new employer-designed standards and some of the limitations and criticisms of the previous apprenticeship frameworks. In chapter two, we explored the importance of ensuring training programmes are comprehensively planned and designed to build on a robust understanding of apprentices' starting points. On- and off-the-job training should be carefully sequenced and complement each other, to challenge and support apprentices to develop the significant and substantial new knowledge, skills and behaviours they need to develop to secure occupational competency and fully meet the needs of employers.

In chapter three, we explored what 'learning' is and how topics, concepts and knowledge need to be delivered in manageable chunks, building on prior knowledge and experience. New material needs to be carefully managed to ensure learners are not overloaded but sufficiently challenged to think hard and build new connections in their long-term memory. We explored the role of technology to engage apprentices and provide opportunities for self-paced learning before and after training sessions. In chapter four, we unpicked different types and methods of assessment and the need to provide specific but challenging feedback on the task *and* process of learning.

In the previous chapter, we have explored the need for trainers, learners, assessors, coaches and employers to come together regularly to rigorously and meaningfully review the progress of apprentices in the widest sense, to make adaptations and to signpost support where required. We investigated different coaching and mentoring techniques to support apprentices to overcome barriers to their learning and work towards clear and challenging targets and action plans.

Enhancing the quality of apprenticeships

It is important to ensure that these key guiding principles are put in place throughout an apprenticeship programme to ensure it continues to provide a high-quality standard of education. Training providers will need to put in place a range of internal quality assurance (IQA) mechanisms to regularly monitor, standardise and review the quality and impact of their provision on the learning journey, making timely enhancements and adaptations where required. This process of continuous self-assessment could consider a patchwork of evidence from a range of different sources, such as feedback from apprentices, their employers, trainers and coaches, reviews of training and progress reviews in action, scrutiny of the quality and standard of learners' work over time, standardisation events and activities, and analysis of key data and other performance indicators (Figure 6.1).

Ongoing review and analysis of performance data will help organisations to update their quality improvement actions plans, which will help them to identify, monitor and manage actions and interventions that will have a positive impact on the quality of education and the apprentices' experience. Improvement actions may also be informed by the outcomes of external quality assurance processes, for example feedback from awarding organisations and regulators.

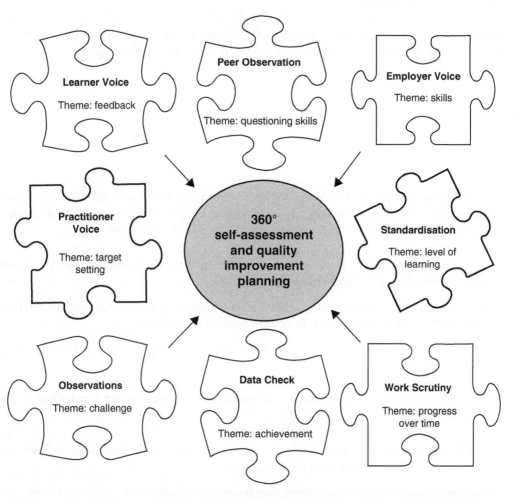

Figure 6.1 A patchwork of performance evidence to inform self-assessment

Education inspection framework

As we explored in chapter one, Ofsted carried out quality assurance activities to report on the overall effectiveness of apprenticeship provision. When carrying out full inspection, inspectors will make graded judgements in the following areas:

- overall effectiveness

- the quality of education

- behaviour and attitudes

- personal development

- leadership and management

Inspectors use a four-point grading scale to make all judgements, including, where applicable, on the effectiveness of the different types of provision offered, for example apprenticeships:

- grade 1: outstanding

- grade 2: good

- grade 3: requires improvement

- grade 4: inadequate

As well as carrying out full and short inspections, new apprenticeship providers also receive an Ofsted monitoring visit within 24 months of first being funded by the ESFA. Monitoring visits assess a provider's progress in delivery of quality apprenticeships in three main themes:

(1) How much progress have **leaders** made in ensuring that the provider is meeting all the requirements of successful apprenticeship provision?

(2) What progress have leaders and managers made in ensuring that apprentices benefit from **high-quality training** that leads to positive outcomes for apprentices?

(3) How much progress have leaders and managers made in ensuring that effective **safeguarding arrangements** are in place?

Each theme receives an overall judgement at the end of the visit, and a report is published on the Ofsted website:

- **insufficient** progress: progress has been either slow or insubstantial or both, and the demonstrable impact on learners has been negligible

- **reasonable** progress: the provider's actions are already having a beneficial impact on learners, and improvements are sustainable and are based on the provider's thorough quality assurance procedures

- **significant** progress: progress has been rapid and is already having considerable beneficial impact on learners.

New providers will then normally receive a full inspection within 24 months of the publication of the monitoring visit report, unless one of more of the judgements is graded as insufficient, in which case a follow-up visit or full inspection will take place much earlier. Ofsted reports help students, employers and parents to understand how a provider is operating and the quality of their educational provision. Where the quality of education is found to be inadequate, this can have serious funding implications for the provider, who may find their ESFA funding contract is withdrawn.

Therefore, it is critical that apprentices are recruited with integrity onto appropriate programmes that help them develop and progress. Providers will need to ensure that teaching and training is high quality and designed to meet apprentice's needs. Employers will need to ensure that they understand the purpose and requirements of an apprenticeships as an education and training route and make sure this is the most appropriate way to develop staff undertaking an apprenticeship programme.

FIND OUT MORE

Ofsted makes their judgements against a published education inspection framework (EIF) and an inspection handbook relating to further education and skills. These documents outline what inspectors will look for when making judgements on how well the curriculum meets the principles and requirements of an apprenticeship:

- Evidence will include the extent to which the provider's staff engage with employers to:
  - complete the apprenticeship commitment statement
  - plan the initial assessment, training, assessments, review points and milestones throughout
  - agree any additional qualifications to be included
  - monitor and support apprentices, including those with SEND and those who have high needs, to progress quickly, gain new knowledge, skills and behaviours and achieve to their full potential.
- Inspectors will judge how well trainers, assessors, coaches and mentors communicate up-to-date vocational and technical subject knowledge that reflects expected industry practice and meets employers' needs.
- Inspectors will determine whether apprentices acquire that knowledge effectively so that they demonstrate the required skills and behaviours that enable them to complete their apprenticeships, contribute to their workplace and fulfil their career aims by progressing to their intended job roles or other sustained employment, promotion or, where appropriate, moving to a higher level of apprenticeship or qualification.
- Inspectors will also consider whether arrangements for safeguarding young people and vulnerable learners are appropriate and effective.

Download the Ofsted EIF and further education and skills inspection handbook: www.apprenticeships. today/ofsted. Now think about how you would define and describe a 'good' standard of education.

Explore the grade descriptors for each of the different judgement areas. What might this mean for you and your apprentices?

Evaluating the impact of training

Many providers engage in a process of work scrutiny to explore how well their apprentices are progressing and to make judgements on the impact of education and training on learners' knowledge and skills. Work scrutiny helps to explore if occupational standards are being met or exceeded and if learners are operating at the correct level for their programme. For example, apprentices may be producing regular, detailed evidence, which is well presented and organised, but it may be overly descriptive and lacking in criticality, analysis and evaluation; the key cognitive skills often are required at the higher levels. Apprentice's practical work may be simplistic and rudimentary, lacking the precision and accuracy required by the occupational standard. When evaluating examples of learner work, it may be useful to compare examples at two or more different checkpoints, to see if apprentices are responding to feedback and making progress over time. It may be useful to consider some of the following prompts.

- What improvements are noted between the two examples in apprentices' occupational and vocational knowledge, skills and understanding?

- Is the work accurate, up to date, and at the appropriate level for the standard of apprenticeship?

- Are there examples of progress in apprentices' applied literacy, numeracy and ICT skills? Are SPaG errors still being made repeatedly?

- How well does the standard of work relate to the learner's individual assessments and targets?

- How helpful, specific and constructive is the trainer's marking, assessment and feedback? Have learners acted on it to improve?

- Does the evidence demonstrate apprentices' pride in their work and wider skills development, e.g. study skills, research skills, referencing and presentation?

Where scrutiny and evaluation of learners' work raises concerns about the quality of training, the support for learners or the standard of evidence, specific training may be necessary to address any systemic quality concerns quickly, ensuring that apprentices are receiving the high quality of education and care they deserve.

Continuous professional development

Ongoing quality improvement and enhancement will almost certainly involve regular staff training and development. A CPD programme should be both proactive and reactive. For example, development activities can be planned in advance to ensure upcoming changes in legislation or working practices, sector developments and professional updating all take place. The CPD programme should also be responsive to the outcomes of internal and external quality assurance activities, reacting to emerging actions, themes and common areas for development. Training and enhancement activities could be targeted for an individual practitioner where a development need is identified, or where a particular theme for improvement is identified across a number of practitioners or departments, training activities could be offered across the organisation.

Where time and funding for professional development is limited, organisations may need to prioritise training and support where it is needed the most (Figure 6.2).

Essential

- Essential mandatory training that is required to ensure that operations are safe and providers are meeting all their staturoty and regulated requirements.
- For example: Safeguarding, 'Prevent', first aid, health and safety, equality and diversity, awarding body approval requiements.

Priority

- Key development activities and training to ensure trainers' subject expertise and pedagocial knowledge is developed, and the needs of apprentices are well met.
- For example: teaching, learning and assessment, embedding English and maths, questioning skills, effective use of EdTech, how to challenge learners, coaching and mentoring.

Enhancement

- High quality providers will also offer additional enhancement training that promotes the sharing of best practice, collaboration and inspirational delivery.
- For example: 'back-to-the-floor' industry days, research events, peer collaboration and lesson study, achievement of higher-level qualifications.

Figure 6.2 Prioritisation of training

Vocational and pedagogical enhancement

Apprenticeship providers should ensure that tutors, trainers and coaches receive focussed and highly effective professional development. As well as focussing on trainers' subject, vocational and technical knowledge and expertise, this should also develop and enhance their pedagogical knowledge. As we explored in chapter three, keeping up to date with education research and thinking will help trainers and coaches to prioritise their time and resources on approaches and strategies that are more likely to have a positive impact on apprentices and their learning. This could be achieved by a mix of 'hard' and 'soft', or 'formal' and 'informal' CPD activities, as shown in Table 6.1.

Table 6.1 Types of CPD activities

More formal CPD activities	Less formal CPD activities
• Attending a planned training event or webinar. This may be led by a subject or pedagogical expert and may include certification of attendance. • Completing a formal qualification which is assessed and certified to set standards, either through online learning, attendance at face-to-face sessions or a blended approach.	• Following educational thinkers, researchers, authors and practitioners on social media, such as Twitter. • Reading key educational texts and journals that link research and practice. • Watching YouTube clips and TED talks on teaching, learning and assessment topics.

Vocational, technical and sector specific knowledge and skills may also be maintained through formal and informal methods, but also through regular industry days where trainers and tutors complete professional placements or work shadowing within the occupational area they are supporting. This helps to ensure they remain current and credible and can develop apprentices' skills in line with modern industry practices.

Qualifications for quality

Those working with apprentices can follow a number of specific training routes themselves, including their own apprenticeship routes, as seen in Table 6.2.

Table 6.2 Apprenticeships for those working with apprentices

Apprenticeship standard	Who is it for?	Typical duration to gateway:
Level 3 Learning Mentor Apprenticeship	For those supporting learners of all ages, and all levels, to develop within a new work role.	12 months
Level 4 Assessor Coach Apprenticeship	For those coaching and assessing vocational learners, usually on a one-to-one basis, in a range of learning environments.	15 months
Level 5 Learning and Skills Teacher	For those teaching young people and adults within all parts of the education and training sector.	24 months
Level 7 Academic Professional	For those working within the higher education (HE) sector delivering higher education teaching.	18 months

In addition, a range of short qualifications also support the role of those planning, delivering, assessing and quality assuring the new employer-designed apprenticeship standard, for example:

• Level 3 Award in Understanding the Principles and Practices of Assessment

• Level 3 Award in Assessing Competence in the Work Environment

• Level 3 Award in Understanding End-Point Assessment

• Level 4 Award in Understanding the Internal Quality Assurance of Assessment Processes and Practice

• Level 4 Certificate in Leading the Internal Quality Assurance of Assessment Processes and Practice

Harnessing EdTech for CPD

Recent years has seen a significant surge in the so-called 'research-ed' movement, to encourage educators to use instructional methods, approaches and strategies that are based on evidence. It is well worth exploring the latest popular educational titles to keep up to date with the latest thinking of effective pedagogy. One efficient way to stay on top of current developments in pedagogy and with the apprenticeship landscape is to follow useful practitioners, organisations and groups on social media platforms such as Twitter. Some useful examples to consider are shown in Table 6.3.

A large range of free online courses are also now available through the so-called 'MOOC revolution': Massive Open Online Courses. MOOCs are online courses available to all, often provided by some of the world's leading universities. They provide a mix of teaching, learning activities and assessments, in a whole range of subject areas, sometimes with the option to achieve accreditation and certification for an administration fee. MOOCs can provide a convenient way to undertake vocational, technical and pedagogical professional development in a convenient format. Examples of popular MOOC providers include those shown in Table 6.4.

Table 6.3 Social media connections using Twitter

Twitter accounts	
• @researchED1	researchED is a teacher-led organisation designed to bridge the gap between research and practice in education.
• @feresearchmeet	An open group for building and supporting engagement with research in FE, led by practitioners, for practitioners.
• @AELPUK	The Association of Employment and Learning Providers represents 900 providers delivering apprenticeships, skills and jobs.
• @FEWeek	In-depth, investigative journalism, for the FE & Skills Sector.
• @WALKTHRUs_5	Teaching Walkthrus are 5-step guides for instructional coaching by @teacherhead and @OliCav
• @SocietyET	The Society for Education and Training (SET) is the membership body dedicated to professionals working across FE, vocational teaching and training.
• @TeacherToolkit	Ross Morrison McGill and the resources shared via @TeacherToolkit have reached over 13 million people in every country around the world.
• @worldskillsuk	WorldSkills UK is an independent charity and partnership between employers, education and governments, to raise standards in apprenticeships and technical education.
Twitter Hashtags	
• #FEResearchMeet • #JoyFE • #ideasroom • #APConnect	Hashtags provide a way to easily search for tweets on a particular theme or by members of a group. Start searching to join in with like-minded practitioners and be prepared to ask questions, get thinking, make connections and learn new ideas.

Table 6.4 Four examples of MOOC providers

Coursera www.coursera.org	One of the most popular platforms, Coursera provides hundreds of free courses which gives learners access to on-demand video lectures, homework exercises and discussion forums. Paid courses provide a shareable Course Certificate upon completion.
FutureLearn www.futurelearn.com	Founded in 2012, FutureLearn is a partnership between the Open University and SEEK Ltd, offering free courses from a range of UK and international universities and organisations in a broad range of subjects including business, health care, IT, engineering, maths, study skills and teaching.
OpenLearn www.open.edu/ openlearn	Launched in 2006, OpenLearn is the home of free learning from the Open University, offering over 900 short courses, ranging from 1 to 100 hours of study.
edX www.edX.org	Founded by Harvard and MIT, edX has a mission to increase access to high-quality education for everyone, everywhere. EdX is home to more than 20 million learners.

Being professional

Undertaking ongoing training and professional development is certainly part of what it takes to be a professional but what else? Professionalism means different things to different people, from being punctual and presentable, to following guidelines and policies and keeping up to date. The Education and Training Foundation (ETF) is responsible for setting and maintaining the professional standards and code of practice for those working in the further education (FE) and skill sector. The standards were developed in 2014 in consultation with practitioners and providers from across the sector. Based around three key pillars of values and attributes, knowledge and understanding, and skills, the twenty standards provide a clear shared set of expectations of what it means to be a professional working in the sector, including:

• teachers and trainers are reflective and enquiring practitioners who think critically about their own educational assumptions, values and practices

• they draw on relevant research as part of evidence-based practice

• they act with honesty and integrity to maintain high standards of ethics and professional behaviour in support of learners and their expectations

• teachers and trainers are subject and/or vocational specialists as well as experts in teaching and learning

• they are committed to maintaining and developing their expertise in both aspects of their role to ensure the best outcomes for their learners.

The purpose of the standards is to support teachers and trainers to maintain and improve standards of teaching and learning, and outcomes for learners.

FIND OUT MORE

The ETF provide a useful self-assessment to help practitioners understand how well they are currently performing against the professional standards. This is a useful starting point to identify areas for professional development and to provide a national reference point that organisations can use to support the ongoing development of their staff.

Find out more and complete the self-assessment tool at: www.et-foundation.co.uk/supporting/professional-standards

---

TAKE IT FURTHER

For those practitioners successfully achieving a qualification at level 5, the ETF offer a route to Qualified Teacher Learning and Skills Teacher (QTLS), professional recognition status which is equivalent to the Qualified Teacher Status (QTS) for those primarily working in the school sector.

Launched in 2017, the Advanced Teacher Status (ATS) programme offers an accreditation route which demonstrates advanced professionalism and mastery in FE and training. ATS holders are also automatically conferred Chartered Teacher Status, raising the status and parity of apprenticeship professionals working across the sector.

To find out more about QTLS and ATS, including eligibility criteria, visit https://set.et-foundation.co.uk/professionalism

---

Working with others

Professional standard 20 highlights how professional teachers and trainers 'contribute to organisational development and quality improvement through collaboration with others'. It is essential that tutors, trainers, coaches and those carrying out IQA roles work together to improve the quality of provision for apprentices, for example:

- trainers could carry out peer observations to share best practice, pick up new ideas and see how others approach their delivery and management of the learning environment

- colleagues carrying out IQA roles will review examples of learner work and tutor's assessment and feedback, to ensure that appropriate standards are met and any awarding organisation requirements are adhered to

- trainers, coaches, Functional Skills and ALS staff should meet together to see how apprentices' holistic needs can be met across the programme in a joined-up manner, rather than as a series of separate functions

- practitioners can learn from others working in different organisations and contexts to learn lessons from those more experienced with new standards or EPA arrangements.

Learning from other apprenticeship stakeholders

Six experienced apprenticeship professionals and stakeholders now generously offer us an invaluable insight into the world of new apprenticeship standards, their purpose, how they can be best designed and implemented. They steer us to key considerations and priorities to help guide, shape and influence our professional work in this sector.

Voice 1: Jo Brodrick – Head of Apprenticeships Walsall College

Jo explores the impact of three driving forces on the apprenticeship landscape: funding, the curriculum and assessment.

The world of Further Education and Skills is in a constant state of change, and for those of us involved in apprenticeships this has been amplified in recent years into a sense of a world 'turned upside down'. Apprenticeships are not what they were and not what the vast majority of the public thinks they are. In fact, public misconception remains a key barrier to apprenticeships gaining the traction required for our apprentices, employers, communities and the economy to realise the full potential that apprenticeships offer.

So why is our world 'turned upside down'? Three key fundamental things have changed: how we are funded, what we teach and how our apprentices are assessed. The shift from a system wholly funded through allocations dictated by government departments and given to providers, to a more meaningful employer-led funding system has meant engagement with employers is even more critical. When providers were the funding holders too many employers disengaged from the training to the extent that some made little attempt to attend progress reviews. This led apprentices to frequently identify their learning as almost separate from their job. Like train tracks, they run alongside each other but don't overlap.

However, the very best apprenticeships are where training is planned and delivered collaboratively. Where learning is applied, practised, developed and finally mastered at work. With the changes to apprenticeship funding, more employers are beginning to shift their thinking, and as a result, joint planning and reviews are more common. This supports apprentices to effectively apply learning to their job and make better progress at work.

The fact that many employers now hold the purse strings creates new dynamics between provider and employer and requires careful navigation to manage the push and pull that sometimes occurs. It can also cause internal issues for employers where levy spend becomes a key performance indicator over and above the effectiveness of apprenticeship training. For example; a training provider may have specific entry criteria for an apprenticeship based on the very best interest of the apprentice, whilst the employer (the purse holder) wants a whole group of staff to be included in a programme regardless of prior learning or initial assessment results. It takes a brave provider to say no to the one apprentice putting at risk a whole cohort but a sensible one to be clear with the employer on their reason, stand their ground and offer alternative training and development for the one who might miss out.

Apprenticeship standards

Many providers who transitioned early onto apprenticeship standards (encouraged by more favourable funding) tried to replicate a qualification structure and introduced units and assessments often found in traditional NVQs. This practice provided a comfort blanket for employers, providers, tutors and assessors. It led to a focus on criteria based summative assessment rather than effective coaching and rich formative assessment to develop apprentices to achieve well in their end-point assessment and progress within their chosen career.

It is easy to see why everyone involved might be nervous of this transition. With frameworks, measuring progress has been inextricably linked with completing units and meeting assessment criteria. Employers are comfortable and familiar with the model, many having been trained that way themselves. In turn providers have used these measures to monitor the effectiveness of their trainers and ensure timely progress and achievement. Standards require us all to think differently, plan differently, deliver differently, monitor progress differently and measure staff performance differently.

End-point assessment

The end-point assessment provides a 'snap shot' holistic assessment of the learner's skills, similar to an industry trade test. This causes a challenge as the language of being 'qualified' is closely tied to the completion of a traditional qualification. Taking some time before completing an apprenticeship is seen as qualification enough. Many end-point assessments demand that apprentices demonstrate their ability to apply years of learning under extreme pressure, observed by a stranger. For those with longer practical assessments this is akin to taking your driving test for a whole day. Yet despite this enormous pressure the vast majority who undertake their EPA pass, and large numbers achieve high grades, testament to their hard work and the support of the employer and training provider. This level of rigour is not widely understood and therefore is currently underappreciated. As the final transition to standards has taken place one can only hope that over time it becomes recognised, and apprenticeships, especially those at Level 2 and Level 3, are no longer seen as the poor relation to more 'academic' routes.

The transformation of public understanding of what an apprenticeship is and who apprentices are will be a slow process. However, as those who undertake apprenticeships now become the decision-makers of the future, perception will shift. When will we know it has happened? When employers ask one simple question of every vacancy they have and say: 'Why not an apprentice?'

REFLECTION POINT

Jo identifies the shifting structure and status of apprenticeships, and some of the key implications for providers and employers of managing the move from frameworks to standards.

- What has the impact of this transition been on your role and working practices?
- How can training providers and employers work together to ensure they are recruiting apprentices with integrity?

Voice 2: Professor Vicky Duckworth – Edge Hill University

Vicky talks about the transformative power of FE and how her research with Dr. Rob Smith aims to understand and provide evidence of how the FE sector is vital in transforming lives and communities in twenty-first century Britain.

Further education is often marginalised by policy. Indeed, as everyone who works in colleges knows, since 2009, further education in England and the UK has been subjected to deep cuts, and these cuts have gone far beyond anything endured by other sectors of education (Paton, 2010). In effect, these cuts have hurt the communities that colleges serve and have penalised staff who work hard day in and day out to provide transformative teaching and learning experiences.

The 'Transformative Teaching and Learning' project (https://transforminglives.web.ucu.org.uk) offers a way of theorising education and training as a transformative critical space that restores students' hope and agency. Learners, apprentices and tutors had the opportunity to tell their stories, and the impact it has on individuals, society and the economy.

Dean, an apprentice, offers an insight into how a transformative teaching and learning environment could meet an employer's needs while also acting as a catalyst for personal and professional development. In Dean's case, his employer liaised closely with the college to ensure a construction curriculum that was appropriate. The employer relied absolutely on the expertise and the affirmative approaches adopted by the tutors. Dean arrived at college with few formal qualifications but with years of experience of labouring on building sites. His opportunities have opened up since returning to college as an apprentice. For Dean, attending college also meant overcoming the significant barrier of a lack of self-confidence. Dean explains that:

> Given the opportunity to further myself, that's a no brainer. But then coming to college, that first day, I was like: I'm not sure I can do this…. It's changed me. I can do things. I am capable…The first day I started I had no computer skills… Now I feel like I've got a bit of respect. It's definitely life-changing… Even with the kids, I went to parents' evening… I ended up chatting (to the teacher) more about me than about (my daughter)…. I've been promoted to be a site manager. It's been an amazing turnaround.

Simon, the managing director of a construction company and Dean's employer, spoke about the importance of 'growing' and 'supporting' his own talent. By this he meant positioning learning at the heart of his company. This involved him in developing a holistic educational experience with a local college that blurred the boundaries between learning spaces and the workplace. The apprenticeship course that Dean was undertaking was dependent on Simon's personal commitment as an employer to his employees. Simon saw construction as a vocation and a career with opportunities for personal growth and the development of skills and knowledge.

Simon expressed that:

> I've built a five year course – when people say an apprenticeship, (normally) it's two years. I've been absolutely saddened by the attitude of the industry where it is encouraged and rewarded to collect as many apprentices as you can, massive intake then after two years, you take an eighteen year old and you say: I'm sorry there's no future with us…. The driving force for us is, you pass and do your apprenticeship with us and you are guaranteed a career. That's part of the deal… you work hard for me, you work hard for the business and we will look after you and we will guarantee you a framework.

Simon's non-exploitative approach is distinctive and, in the transformative teaching and learning experiences on offer through his model of apprenticeship, he seeks to connect the success of his company with the personal development of employees. In his case, there is space alongside the learner and the teacher on the 'driving seat' and his is an enabling rather than a dominant role.

FIND OUT MORE

Find out more about the UCU Transforming lives and communities research project, which aims to understand and provide evidence of how the FE sector is vital in transforming lives and communities in twenty-first century Britain. The study provided students, teachers, parents and employers with the opportunity to tell their stories, linking the distinctness of FE to the impact it has on individuals, society and the economy, and strongly drawing out the role of the teacher in making a difference to quality teaching and learning.

www.apprenticeships.today/transformativelives

REFLECTION POINTS

- Vicky highlights the transformative power of apprentice's and FE on people's lives. How is your work with your apprentices having an impact on their professional and personal lives?
- How can more employers take the approach of Simon, in recruiting and investing in their apprentice's journey with integrity, providing them with a secure path to long-term employment?

Voice 3: Clive Cheetham – Quality Improvement Manager, National Independent Training Provider

Clive explores the key challenges and opportunities of maintaining high-quality provision when moving from apprenticeship frameworks to standards.

Apprenticeships develop the knowledge, skills and behaviours that are needed to produce a competent workforce that enhances both productivity and personal development, and therefore contributing to the economy. They have an element of transferrable skills in recognition of providing longer-term currency in an ever-changing economy. Apprenticeships support growth at individual, local, regional and national levels. The transition from frameworks to standards has been very demanding given the significant fundamental changes to content and support infrastructure. The key differences for us include significant changes to staff responsibilities, and the direct involvement of specialist staff, to ensure the standards are not only delivered, but closely monitored and evidence collated.

With the new apprenticeships, learners' retention of the knowledge elements are now more important to ensure they are able to explain its impact on their job role to the end-point assessor, for example how they apply their technical knowledge to improve their performance. Technical qualifications are no longer a compulsory element of apprenticeship standards; however, we have developed a new BTEC qualification that maps into the standard, which we believe not only improves the whole experience while on programme but also offers additional future opportunities for later life.

End-point assessment (EPA) methods are more robust and broader than framework achievement requirements. They include a multiple-choice knowledge test, practical observation and 90-minute professional discussion, supported by a portfolio of evidence. So apprentices are tested, for the first time, on their technical on-the-job abilities, unlike with the old frameworks. EPA is also carried out independently, so unlike previously, apprentices will be faced with strangers who will decide if they have passed or not, which may be more daunting for them. We therefore need to invest further time in preparing them for this. Planning and regular assessment will be more critical in ensuring they are ready for EPA.

As with frameworks, I am not sure I agree with the continued requirement that apprentices must achieve the English and maths qualifications at level 2, to enter the EPA Gateway, given that learners will have had 11 years of being taught through the school system. The relatively low post-16 retake results seem to support this view. Why should an apprentice, who is otherwise successful in their chosen career that does not require such qualifications, be penalised? Perhaps the requirement to develop wider, everyday English and maths is more productive.

Regular dialogue, especially at the beginning and early stages of the programme, is essential to ensure apprenticeships are of a high quality and meet the needs of the employers. We need to ensure consistency in how we measure apprentices' attainment against the standards and specifications. Careful monitoring will need to take place and feedback will need to be specific, especially if gaps are identified. Quality assurance can also be formally carried out through quality checks and visits that cover the requirements of the standards, but also evaluate all the expectations of excellent apprenticeship provision, such as apprentices' personal development, safeguarding, equality, diversity and inclusion, British values, and the wider development of apprentice's English and maths skills. These quality checks will involve work scrutiny, record-keeping, observation and discussions with apprentices and employer staff, to ensure evaluations are based on robust evidence.

We were part of the trailblazer group alongside our employers, all of whom have all been consulted with and involved in the development of the new standards. Together, high-quality staff, regular communication and a range of quality assurance mechanisms help to ensure high-quality apprenticeship provision.

REFLECTION POINT

- Clive identifies the importance of well-qualified and highly experienced staff, along with frequency and wide-ranging quality assurance activities, as a key aspect of delivering high-quality apprenticeships. What do you see as the most important aspects for ensuring apprentices receive an excellent standard of education and training?

- How do you feel about the requirement for apprentices to achieve minimum standards in formal English and maths qualifications, as part of their training programme? Should this be a requirement for learners who have not already achieved this formal level of accreditation?

Voice 4: Sue Martin – Education Consultant

Sue explores the key role of initial and formative assessment in meeting the needs of apprentices and preparing them for end-point assessment.

Apprenticeships are a wonderful opportunity for a learner to move into the world of work and learn new skills in a job while being supported by an experienced employer. The employer is a critical partner and will help to design the learning programme to meet the needs of their business. The essential ingredient in making the apprenticeship a success is to make sure there is a team approach to initial assessment. The trainer/coach should record what the apprentice already knows, can do and fully understands. There is nothing more demoralising for a learner than having to repeat learning they already know. By recognising the (relevant) prior experience of the apprentice there is more chance to keep them engaged, motivated and stretch their knowledge.

Careful and probing questions will need to be used to gain the right amount of information from the apprentice as they may not answer fully, or not understand, the detail of the standard and therefore think they have more knowledge than they actually do. Once the initial assessment has been undertaken then a clear curriculum and training plan can be drawn up and an individualised learning plan agreed. By paying attention to the initial assessment, this will show the comparison and distance travelled at the next on-programme assessment. As the apprentice learns and develops more skills at work they will be able to show how they apply in their role and show more progress in their formative assessments. This will help to demonstrate the impact of the curriculum. Formative assessment is an essential element of supporting an apprentice through their learning experience. Apprentices should receive developmental feedback as this is a powerful way to record progress being made and helps the apprentice to refine their knowledge and skills whilst also building confidence that will affect behaviours in the workplace.

The trainer or coach is a critical role as not only do they support and develop the apprentice, but they also work collaboratively with other professionals who all have a part to play in the success of the apprentice. The coach should be a good communicator as part of their role in ensuring formative and ongoing assessment is effective, for example actively listen, provide clear feedback and agree with the apprentice the next steps of their individualised programme. By involving the apprentice through each step and decision, this will help to keep them motivated and engaged in the learning process.

As the apprentice is formally assessed at the end of the programme, it is even more important there is regular formative assessment throughout the learning plan. By carrying out regular assessment, this will help to identify if the apprentice is making the expected progress towards the targets and goals you have agreed. If not, this will allow enough time to put extra support in place or adapt the training plan. If an apprentice has a strong knowledge or skills base in a particular area, a good learning plan would look to test and enhance that throughout the programme, to make sure apprentices are ready to demonstrate this at the end-point assessment.

REFLECTION POINT

- Sue talks about the 'impact of the curriculum'. How do you know that your curriculum is having a positive impact on an apprentice and their abilities to carry out their role effectively?

- Sue highlights the importance of assessors and coaches working collaboratively with other professionals. What access do you have to a range of other professionals that can have an impact on learner's progress and development?

Voice 5: John Daley – Programme Manager, National Training Provider

John reflects on the importance of establishing early effective working relationships with apprentices' employers as a key part of the apprenticeship process.

Apprenticeships provide a direct and effective route into employment which reflect the skills needs and gaps of industry. Programme planning is vital to ensure effective apprenticeship delivery and a positive impact on achievement. Planning should identity suitable curriculum content and consider the most appropriate delivery medium and style. It is important to consider the blend of on- and off-the-job training through the programme, and the sequencing of modules and units, to really maximise the effective partnerships between education providers and employers. I coach senior managers on the Level 5 operations management apprenticeships, and we sequence the curriculum carefully from the start.

For example, I recently worked with an apprentice manager, and their director, to set project activities, theories and tools to explore, in line with the standard and awarding body requirements. I encouraged the apprentice to conduct live business projects in line with their company objectives to help support and address their skills gaps. We reviewed the plan of learning regularly as the program went on, taking onboard feedback for senior directors. This helped to highlight further development needs, for example delegating effectively as production and demand in the organisation increased. We adjusted the theory content accordingly to underpin the learning of key topics, such as how to delegate and improve time management. I also carried out onsite observations to see the apprentice in action. I was able to offer direct coaching to support their work with their team. The observations helped me to spot skills gaps, for example in the apprentice's ability to deal with conflict relating to poor performance of the team. I then supported the apprentice and director to upskill team members, to reduce conflict through improved communication and change management processes.

My advice to any new apprentices, trainers and skills coaches would be to ensure that you are experienced and confident in your own subject area directly related to the needs of the apprenticeship standard. You need to use all the initial assessment, diagnostic tools and tests to fully understand what the apprentice already knows, what their skills level is currently at, to identify any skills gaps, and to establish how they respond to academic development. You then need to establish a close relationship with the apprentice's direct mentor and employer. This is critical in order to establish a positive learning and training culture with the organisation.

The skills coach should display an open, supportive, flexible and honest approach to connect with the apprentice and deal with any potential learning barriers early on in the programme. They need to be proactive in being a voice and advocate for the apprentice, to ensure they get the support and resources they need in the workplace. The apprentice needs support from the coach to understand and set their own targets, identifying how they can reach their individual goals in an achievable way. The apprentice needs to see and feel small successes along the journey, both academically and operationally, in the workplace. Therefore, the coach needs to be close to the employment activity to help recognise opportunities for success and progression.

REFLECTION POINT

- John talks about the importance of establishing an effective rapport with apprentices' employers as soon as possible. How do you work with busy managers and employers to establish this working relationship?
- John highlights the needs to be a voice, or advocate, for the apprentice if they need additional support or resources from their workplace when completing their apprenticeship. How would you approach this constructively with the employers you are working with, to ensure the apprentice gets what they need?

Voice 6: Jenny Coogan – Business Administration Manger, Secure Care Birmingham and Solihull Mental Health NHS Foundation Trust

Jenny talks about her recent experience of being an adult apprentice, completing the level 5 departmental manager apprenticeship.

For me, there are two different aspects to being an adult apprentice. Firstly, the word 'apprentice'; this word always conjures up a young person who is starting their career. I do not think of this word and think of a 40 something (no I am not divulging) experienced professional. It has been many years since I took my first steps into work and was called the junior. It was daunting to me to admit to others that I was an apprentice; surely if I had thoughts like this they did too. At times I was embarrassed and a little shy about announcing I was an 'apprentice'.

The second major feeling it brought out in me was the fear of attending college again, the fear of starting to learn again at my age, and with the commitments I have in life now. Not only do I have a full-time job, a partner and two children (one of who has additional needs), I now want to take on a level 5 course! The first time I attended the college and saw the young people starting on their career paths I was a little envious, but also terrified one of them was going to think I was a member of staff and start asking me questions! I felt like a total fraud standing there with my lanyard and bag full of books. Since leaving school, I have done the odd course over the years but nothing to this level. Don't even get me started on my levels of anxiety the first time I had to write an essay.

However, I have to say over the last two years, with the support of my personal tutor, none of these anxieties have come true. I have never been chased off the campus as a fraud, and my essays have been marked and passed. I even went on to pass my maths which is a whole other story. My confidence in my ability to learn, to diversify, and in myself, has grown immensely. I am happy to say that I now proudly tell everyone I am an apprentice and promote this fabulous way of learning. To date, no one has ever laughed at my age, but instead show a real interest in the course and how they could also benefit from this scheme.

To understand how this has impacted my professional development you need to know a little of my past. At age 16, I got my first job as an office junior. From here, I spent the next ten years working my way up to personal assistant to the chief executives. Although I have held many varied roles and have enjoyed my career, I always felt that I was not good enough to be a manager or supervise staff. It was my job to minute meetings, not speak out in them and put my thoughts forward. When I started working in my current organisation, they saw the potential in me and over the space of three years I went from a PA to administration lead, supervising three staff. This started to build my confidence that I could be a competent manager. With this newfound confidence, I enrolled to complete the level five course with Walsall College. After I was accepted onto the course, I applied for a promotion and was successful. One of the key reasons for my successful was my position on the apprenticeship.

My new role means that I manage many staff over multiple sites. This has presented massive challenges for me in terms of communication and time management. By completing the apprenticeship, working with my learning group and personal tutor, it have been able to learn techniques and skills to cope with a whole host of different managerial, HR, and staffing issues that have been thrown at me. If I had not completed this apprenticeship, I would have struggled to find this support, and the safe space it offers to learn on the job and have the opportunity to discuss real life issues and learn the best approaches to deal with them.

One of the main personal challenges was my lack of confidence in my own abilities, about what I could learn and how I would manage my time. The apprenticeship allowed me to reflect and engage in counselling to overcome this. It has given me the confidence and knowledge that I now understand what being a good manager is and how to implement this. Completing the apprenticeship has shown me how resilient and able I am. With the support of my personal tutor and my employer, my anxieties have not come to fruition. I have found that I quite enjoy doing research, writing essays, and putting into practice the practical lessons learnt. I would not be where I am now without the support, guidance and education from the college and my personal tutor. I am now part of the senior managers and leadership team in my organisation and am always open new opportunities. I now sit and discuss my ideas in meetings – not just minute them!

REFLECTION POINT

- Jenny talks about the wider perceptions of apprenticeships and who they are suitable for. To what extent do you feel employers and employees understand the transformative power of apprenticeship programmes for learners of all ages and backgrounds?

- Jenny speaks passionately about the impact of her own apprenticeship programme and the high levels of support she received from the college and her personal tutor. How can you ensure that your apprentices maximise the impact the apprenticeship programme can have on them and their futures?

Final thoughts

Hearing from those involved in the new apprenticeships, it is clear to see how they can have a significant, transformative impact on apprentices and their employers. The transition from apprenticeship frameworks to standards provides a number of challenges as providers, employers, trainers, coaches and learners get to grips with new ways of working, a revised curriculum, radically different assessment arrangements, and new funding systems

The new apprenticeships also offer a valuable opportunity to refocus on learning and progress, not paperwork and tick lists. On high-quality education and training, not on evidence collection and badging of existing skills. They promote the development of real and substantial new competencies, powerful knowledge and impactful workplace behaviours fit for the twenty-first century.

A summary of key points

In this chapter we have looked at a number of key themes:

- the key considerations in planning and delivering high-quality apprenticeships

- the importance of CPD and robust quality assurance

- what it is to be a professional working with the new apprenticeships

- how we can work and learn from others.

Key links

Institute for Apprenticeships and Technical Education www.apprenticeships.today/quality	Guidance from the IATE on how to deliver high-quality apprenticeships, including quality indicators.
Education and Training Foundation www.apprenticeships.today/ETF	The apprenticeship support programme from the ETF provides a collection of resource to support EPA and employer engagement.
Amazing Apprenticeships www.amazingapprenticeships.com	Amazing Apprenticeships is a leading organisation in the education sector, founded to tackle misconceptions about apprenticeships and promote the benefits.
Department for Education www.gov.uk/government/publications/ apprenticeship-accountability-statement	The apprenticeship accountability statement sets out the responsibilities of each organisation with a role in regulating the apprenticeships system.

▬ FURTHER READING ▬

Bradbury, A. and Wynne, V. (2021) *The Apprentice's Guide to End Point Assessment*. Los Angeles, CA: Learning Matters.

Institute for Apprenticeships and Technical Education (2019) *What is a Quality Apprenticeship?* Available at: www.instituteforapprenticeships.org/quality/what-is-a-quality-apprenticeship

Ofsted (2020) *Further Education and Skills Inspection Handbook*. Crown Copyright.

Tummons, J. (2019) *PCET: Learning and Teaching in the Post Compulsory Sector*. London: Learning Matters.

REFERENCES

Alred, G., Garvey, B. and Smith, R. (1998) *Mentoring Pocketbook*. Alresford: Management Pocketbooks.

Anderson, L. and Krathwohl, A. (2000) Taxonomy of Teaching and Learning: A Revision of Bloom's Taxonomy of Educational Objectives. *Educational Psychology*, 479–480.

Armitage, A. and Cogger, A. (2019) *The New Apprenticeships*. St. Albans: Critical Publishing.

Bjork, R.A. (1994) Memory and Metamemory Considerations in the Training of Human Beings. In J. Metcalfe and A.P. Shimamura (eds.), *Metacognition: Knowing About Knowing* (pp. 185–205). Cambridge, MA: MIT Press.

Black, P. and Wiliam, D. (1999) *Assessment for Learning: Beyond the Black Box*. Cambridge: University of Cambridge, School of Education.

Bloom, B., Englehart, M., Furst, E., Hill, W. and Krathwohl, D. (1956) *Taxonomy of Educational Objectives: The Classification of Educational Goals. Handbook I: Cognitive Domain*. New York, NY; Toronto, ON: Longmans, Green.

Bosanquet, P., Radford, J. and Webster, R. (2016) *The Teaching Assistant's Guide to Effective Interaction: How to Maximise Your Practice*. Abingdon: Routledge.

Briceño, E. (2015) *Mistakes Are Not All Created Equal*. MindsetWorks.com. Available at: https://blog.mindsetworks.com/entry/mistakes-are-not-all-created-equal [Accessed: March 2019].

Coe, R. (2013) Improving Education: A Triumph of Hope Over Experience. Inaugural Lecture of Professor Robert Coe, Durham University, 18 June 2013. Available at: www.cem.org/attachments/publications/ImprovingEducation2013.pdf [Accessed: January 2019].

Commission on Adult Vocational Teaching and Learning (2013) *It's About Work... Excellent Adult Vocational Teaching and Learning*. The summary report of the Commission on Adult Vocational Teaching and Learning. Learning and Skills Improvement Service (LSIS). Available at: https://repository.excellencegateway.org.uk/CAVTL-Its-about-work-Report.pdf/ [Accessed: June 2020].

Csikszentmihalyi, M. (2002) *Flow: The Classic Work on How to Achieve Happiness*. London: Rider.

Department for Business, Innovation and Skills and Department for Education (2012) *Richard Review of Apprenticeships*. Available at: www.gov.uk/government/publications/the-richard-review-of-apprenticeships [Accessed: July 2020].

Department for Business, Innovation and Skills and Department for Education (2015) *Apprenticeships (in England): Vision for 2020*. Available at: www.gov.uk/government/publications/apprenticeships-in-england-vision-for-2020 [Accessed: July 2020].

Department for Business, Innovation and Skills and Department for Education (2016) *Report of the Independent Panel on Technical Education.* Available at: www.gov.uk/government/publications/post-16-skills-plan-and-independent-report-on-technical-education [Accessed: July 2020].

Department for Education (2019) *Apprenticeship Off-the-Job Training: Policy Background and Examples.* Available at: www.gov.uk/government/publications/apprenticeships-off-the-job-training [Accessed: July 2020].

Didau, D. (2016) *What If Everything You Knew About Education Was Wrong?* Wales: Crown House Publishing.

Duckworth, V. and Smith, R. (2017) *UCU Research Transforming Lives and Communities. A National Practitioner Guidance Booklet is Being Developed With a Focus on Transformative Education.*

Duckworth, V. and Smith, R. (2018) Breaking the Triple Lock: Further Education and Transformative Teaching and Learning. *Education + Training*, 1–16. https://doi.org/10.1108/ET-05-2018-0111

Dweck, C. (2012) *Mindset: How You Can Fulfil Your Potential.* London: Robinson Publishing.

Ebbinghaus, H. (1964) *Memory: A Contribution to Experimental Psychology.* New York, NY: Dover.

Education and Skills Funding Agency (2019) *Apprenticeships: Initial Assessment to Recognise Prior Learning.* Available at: www.gov.uk/government/publications/apprenticeships-recognition-of-prior-learning/apprenticeships-initial-assessment-to-recognise-prior-learning [Accessed: July 2020].

Enser, Z. and Enser, M. (2020) *Generative Learning in Action.* Woodbridge: John Catt Educational Limited.

Evans, R. (2011) *Short History of Apprenticeships.* Technical Education Matters. Available at: https://technicaleducationmatters.org/2011/01/06/short-history-of-apprenticeships [Accessed: June 2020].

Faraday, S., Overton, C. and Cooper, S. (2011) *Developing Effective Vocational Teaching and Learning Through Teaching Models: A Guide.* London: LSN.

Field, S. and Windisch, H. (2016) *Building Skills for All: A Review of England: Policy Insights From the Survey of Adult Skills.* OECD. Available at: http://www.oecd.org/education/skills-beyond-school/building-skills-for-all-review-of-england.pdf [Accessed: July 2020].

Fiorella, L. and Mayer, R.E. (2015) *Learning as a Generative Activity: Eight Learning Strategies That Promote Understanding.* New York, NY: Cambridge University Press.

Gagne, R. (1985) *The Conditions of Learning: Training Applications.* New York, NY: Holt, Rinehart and Winston.

Garrison, D.R. and Kanuka, H. (2004) Blended Learning: Uncovering Its Transformative Potential in Higher Education. *Internet and Higher Education*, 7(2), 95–105. Elsevier Ltd. Available at: https://www.learntechlib.org/p/102559/ [Accessed: March 2020].

Harrow, A.J. (1972) *A Taxonomy of the Psychomotor Domain.* New York, NY: David McKay Co.

Hattie, J. (2012) *Visible Learning for Teachers, Maximising Impact on Learning.* Oxford: Routledge.

Hattie, J. and Timperley, H. (2007) The Power of Feedback. *Review of Educational Research*, 77(1), 81–112.

Hymer, B. (2009) *Gifted & Talented Pocketbook*. Alresford: Teachers' Pocketbooks.

Ingle, S. (2020) What is Vocational Learning? In J. Lord (ed.), *Studying Education*. London: Learning Matters.

Ingle, S. and Duckworth, V. (2013a) *Teaching and Training Vocational Learners*. Los Angeles, CA: Learning Matters.

Ingle, S. and Duckworth, V. (2013b) *Enhancing Learning Through Technology in Lifelong Learning: Fresh Ideas; Innovative Strategies*. Maidenhead: Open University Press.

Jones, K. (2019) *Retrieval Practice*. Woodbridge: John Catt Educational Limited.

Kirschner, P. and Hendrick, C. (2020) *How Learning Happens*. New York, NY: Routledge.

Lemov, D. (2015) *Teach Like a Champion 2.0*. San Francisco, CA: Jossey-Bass.

Lovell, O. (2020) *Sweller's Cognitive Load Theory in Action*. Woodbridge: John Cat Education Limited.

Martin, A.J. and Marsh, H.W. (2008) Academic Buoyancy: Towards an Understanding of Students' Everyday Academic Resilience. *Journal of School Psychology*, 46(1), 53–83.

Mirza-Davies, J. (2015) *A Short History of Apprenticeships in England: From Medieval Craft Guilds to the Twenty-First Century*. Available at: https://commonslibrary.parliament.uk/a-short-history-of-apprenticeships-in-england-from-medieval-craft-guilds-to-the-twenty-first-century/ [Accessed: July 2020].

Nuthall, G. (2007) *The Hidden Lives of Learners*. Wellington: NZCER Press.

Oettingen, G. (2015) *Rethinking Positive Thinking: Inside the New Science of Motivation*. New York, NY: Current.

Ofsted (2020) *Further Education and Skills Inspection Handbook*. Crown Copyright.

Panicucci, J. (2007) Cornerstones of Adventure Education. In D. Prouty, J. Panicucci and R. Collinson (eds.), *Adventure Education: Theory and Applications* (pp. 33–48). Champaign, IL: Human Kinetics.

Paton, G. (2010) *Spending Review: Schools Budget Protected*. Available at: https://www.telegraph.co.uk/education/educationnews/8076309/Spending-Review-schools-budget-protected.html [Accessed: March 2020].

Perkins, D. (1992) *Smart Schools: Better Thinking and Learning for Every Child*. New York, NY: Free Press.

Rosenshine, B. (2010) Principles of Instruction. International Academy of Education, UNESCO. Geneva: International Bureau of Education. Available at: www.ibe.unesco.org/fileadmin/user_upload/Publications/Educational_Practices/EdPractices_21.pdf [Accessed: May 2020].

Rosenthal, R. and Jacobsen, L. (1968) *Pygmalion in the Classroom: Teacher Expectation and Pupils' Intellectual Development*. New York, NY: Holt, Rinehart and Winston.

Rowe, M.B. (1986) Wait-Time: Slowing Down May Be a Way of Speeding Up. *Journal of Teacher Education*, 37, 43–50.

Sherrington, T. (2019) *Rosenshine's Principles in Action*. Woodbridge: John Catt Educational Limited.

The Edge Foundation (2019) *Debating the First Principles of English Vocational Education, Volume 2*. London: The Edge Foundation. Available at: https://www.edge.co.uk/sites/default/files/documents/vocational_philosophy_2_final_-_web.pdf. [Accessed: June 2020].

Tolhurst, J. (2010) *The Essential Guide to Coaching and Mentoring*, 2nd ed. London: Pearson Education Limited.

Whitmore, J. (2009) *Coaching for Performance: GROWing Human Potential and Purpose: The Principles and Practice of Coaching and Leadership, People Skills for Professionals*, 4th ed. London: Nicholas Brealey Publishing.

Zenger, J. and Stinnett, K. (2010) *The Extraordinary Coach: How the Best Leaders Help Others Grow*. New York, NY: McGraw-Hill Education.

INDEX